Praise for *KISS YOUR* **FIGHTS** *good-bye*

*"Dr. Turndorf has relationships figured out. If you
want a great relationship, you must follow her
ten-step method for lasting love."*

— **Jack Canfield,** multiple *New York Times*
best-selling author of the *Chicken Soup for the Soul*
series and contributor to *The Secret,* with more
than 500 million books in print

*"If anger and fighting are ruining your dream
of a happy marriage (or relationship), Dr. Turndorf's
conflict-resolution program is for you."*

— **John Gray,** author of the #1 *New York Times* bestseller
Men Are from Mars, Women Are from Venus

*"This well-researched book offers a thorough,
step-by-step program that provides tools for couples
to heal even the most troubled relationships."*

— **Dr. John Mack,** Pulitzer Prize–winning author and
former professor of psychiatry at Harvard Medical School

*"This book is mandatory reading for every couple
that wants to build lasting love."*

— **John Bradshaw,** author of the #1 *New York Times*
bestseller *Homecoming*

KISS
YOUR
FIGHTS
good-bye

ALSO BY DR JAMIE TURNDORF

Love Never Dies: How to Reconnect and Make Peace with the Deceased (available July 2014)*

Make Up Don't Break Up: Dr. Love's Five-Step Plan for Reconciling with Your Ex

The Pleasure of Your Company: A Socio-Psychological Analysis of Modern Sociability (with Emile Jean Pin)

*Available from Hay House

Please visit:

Hay House UK: www.hayhouse.co.uk
Hay House USA: www.hayhouse.com®
Hay House Australia: www.hayhouse.com.au
Hay House South Africa: www.hayhouse.co.za
Hay House India: www.hayhouse.co.in

KISS YOUR FIGHTS

good-bye

DR LOVE'S 10 SIMPLE STEPS TO COOLING CONFLICT AND REKINDLING YOUR RELATIONSHIP

JAMIE TURNDORF, PhD

HAY HOUSE, INC.
Carlsbad, California • New York City
London • Sydney • Johannesburg
Vancouver • Hong Kong • New Delhi

First published and distributed in the United Kingdom by:
Hay House UK Ltd, Astley House, 33 Notting Hill Gate, London W11 3JQ
Tel: +44 (0)20 3675 2450; Fax: +44 (0)20 3675 2451
www.hayhouse.co.uk

Published and distributed in the United States of America by:
Hay House Inc., PO Box 5100, Carlsbad, CA 92018-5100
Tel: (1) 760 431 7695 or (800) 654 5126
Fax: (1) 760 431 6948 or (800) 650 5115
www.hayhouse.com

Published and distributed in Australia by:
Hay House Australia Ltd, 18/36 Ralph St, Alexandria NSW 2015
Tel: (61) 2 9669 4299; Fax: (61) 2 9669 4144
www.hayhouse.com.au

Published and distributed in the Republic of South Africa by:
Hay House SA (Pty) Ltd, PO Box 990, Witkoppen 2068
Tel/Fax: (27) 11 467 8904
www.hayhouse.co.za

Published and distributed in India by:
Hay House Publishers India, Muskaan Complex, Plot No.3, B-2,
Vasant Kunj, New Delhi 110 070
Tel: (91) 11 4176 1620; Fax: (91) 11 4176 1630
www.hayhouse.co.in

Distributed in Canada by:
Raincoast, 9050 Shaughnessy St, Vancouver BC V6P 6E5
Tel: (1) 604 323 7100; Fax: (1) 604 323 2600

A catalogue record for this book is available from the British Library.

ISBN: 978-1-4019-4533-6

*To Jean Pin, my husband
of nearly 30 years, who faithfully
stood beside me through life's ups and
downs. Your love, level of acceptance,
and ongoing devotion to our
relationship are the greatest
gifts of my life.*

CONTENTS

A woman died and appeared before Saint Peter at the gates of heaven.

"What must I do to enter heaven?" the woman asked.

Saint Peter replied, "Very simple. You need only spell one word: *love*."

"That's easy! *L-o-v-e*."

With that, the pearly gates parted and she entered heaven.

Saint Peter then said, "Listen, I have to visit the men's room. Would you watch the gates for me? And remember, if anyone wants to enter, make sure that he or she spells the word."

Saint Peter left, and one minute later, the woman's husband appeared at the gate.

"What are you doing here?" the woman asked.

He replied, "I was so bereft when you died that I died instantly. What do I need to do to get in?"

The woman replied, "It's simple. You just need to spell one word."

"What's the word?" he asked.

"*Czechoslovakia*."

PREFACE
◇◇◇◇◇◇◇◇◇◇◇◇◇◇◇◇◇◇◇◇◇◇◇◇◇

While this book is designed to help husbands and wives resolve chronic fighting, the principles and techniques presented can be applied to unmarried and gay couples, as well as to relationships between parents and children, siblings, and friends.

I also want to make you aware that the generalizations I make about male/female behavior are based upon statistical tendencies. This means that, according to statistical data, a certain behavior is most often displayed by a specific gender. For example, more women than men are emotionally expressive. Don't be surprised if you find that certain generalizations don't fit your particular circumstance. In fact, you may note that your experience is the opposite of a statistical finding. No problem. If you need to reverse the gender in order for my remarks to fit, that's fine. In any case, you will find that the techniques for resolving your conflicts still apply.

You'll also notice that I have addressed many passages of this book to women (the "relationship watchdogs" in our society). Since women tend to notice relationship problems first, they are generally the ones who not only initiate conflict discussions, but also pursue these discussions in an effort to achieve resolution.

As you read on, you will discover that the success of a conflict discussion depends largely on the way in which that discussion is initiated and overseen. For this reason, I spend a good deal of time outlining the ideal and less-than-ideal ways to begin the discussion and see it through to a successful resolution. My recommendations will likely mean that you will need to shift how you handle your conflict discussions.

Many women balk at the idea that they must do all the work. My answer is simple. I don't care if a woman, a man, a hermaphrodite, or a monkey initiates the conflict discussions; all I care about is that your discussions are handled properly. Since it is generally women who take charge of these discussions, we must face the fact that we are already doing the lion's share of the work. Since you're already doing the work, why not do it correctly and effectively?

While your success requires you to make certain shifts, don't think that your partner is getting off scot-free. On the contrary, your partner will be expected to make extraordinary changes in the way he listens and responds to your communications, and by the time you're finished with this program, you'll be amazed by how much he has changed.

On a related note, I want you to be aware that even if the person you are fighting with doesn't engage in the program with you, you will still be able to improve your relationship, even if you are the only one who makes an effort to alter your way of behaving and responding. Like a pebble cast into a pond, your changes alone will have a profound ripple effect upon your relationship. So don't hesitate to roll up your sleeves and be the one to get the ball rolling.

I also want to make you aware of the fact that couples inevitably fall into fighting in response to unmet needs. Anger is the psyche's alarm signal that alerts us to the fact that our emotional needs aren't being met. While angry feelings are the natural by-product of frustrated needs, it's important to know that anger is never the primary emotion. In fact, anger is an emotional smoke screen that conceals the more vulnerable feelings of hurt, sadness, and fear that result from unmet needs.

In my book *Make Up Don't Break Up,* I introduced the concept of Relationship Essential Nutrients to describe the ingredients that a relationship needs to survive and thrive.

Consider the human body: it thrives when it is fed essential nutrients, and it dies when it's deprived of these nutrients. A relationship is no different. If it's not constantly being fed its own essential nutrients, it too disintegrates. When these essential nutrients are missing, or aren't delivered at the right frequency, conflict and fighting overtake the relationship. A relationship cannot survive in the midst of emotional starvation.

Feeding these Relationship Essential Nutrients to each other on a daily basis is key to your relationship survival. As you will soon see, anger and fighting arise in direct proportion to how well you do or don't feed each other. (You will learn more about these nutrients in the section called "The Elements of Relationship Climate Control" in Chapter 7.)

A final note: Although the stories contained in this book are based on true cases, the names have been changed to protect the identities of the people who have shared their lives with me.

INTRODUCTION

◇◇◇

Every couple wants love—endless love. For most of us, love is a joining of the mind and heart, which includes physical attraction, admiration of a partner's personal qualities, and a wish to share together (to hike, swim, watch movies, or what have you). Love also includes a commitment to your beloved's happiness, health, and well-being, as well as a desire to satisfy each other's wishes, needs, requests, and so on. I don't need to continue. You know what love is.

If you're like most people, you loved your mate when you said, "I do." You also vowed to sustain that love "till death do us part." So, why is it that many couples fall out of love? Well, it's because, in spite of their emotional fusion at the beginning of their relationship, lovers constitute two different people whose needs and wishes don't always perfectly match. These differences often lead to overt conflict and fighting over any subject you can imagine, large or small.

Divorce and domestic violence have reached epidemic proportions, and since chronic marital distress is usually a precursor of divorce, and often violence, a program for conflict resolution is needed now more than ever. Millions of conflicted couples, as well as anyone wishing to maintain harmonious relationships, will benefit from my down-to-earth, easy-to-apply program for ending fighting. The escape routes, safety valves, and real answers are basic relationship survival tools.

But don't wait to put these tools to work—fighting only worsens with time. How do I know? I'm popularly known as Dr. Love, and through my Center for Emotional Communication and my website, AskDrLove.com, I have helped millions of couples improve their relationships. In fact, out of my Center, I have spent 30 years conducting observational research with couples suffering from chronic fighting, and my research has produced one of the first proven methods for ending fighting for the majority of people who use it. This book contains the elements of my conflict-resolution program, and if you take the time to apply my principles, you too will break the cycle of destructive fighting.

You may be wondering why you don't already know how to resolve your conflicts. Think about where your formal learning occurred. At school, of course, where you were taught math and English. But what about that course on how to handle your relationships? Zippo. It's a tragedy that no education is offered in this area, considering that almost all of us spend more waking hours in interaction with people than we do performing math calculations.

Isn't it about time we went to love school? Or maybe I should say conflict school, because love and hate are blood relatives; and love cannot survive unless its first cousin, anger, is properly handled. In fact, unresolved anger is the number one killer of love.

Even if your love is on the firing line, if hate and anger are holding your marriage or intimate relationship hostage, don't despair. Contrary to popular belief, you can rekindle the love you felt in the early days of your relationship. But you must work at it. It sounds very unromantic, I know. But leaving your relationship to chance and ending up divorced or estranged is even more unromantic.

A Brief Overview of the Contents of This Book

My program to end relationship fighting begins with a series of preparatory or Cool-Down steps, discussed in Chapters 1 through 7, which must be mastered before you can attempt conflict resolution.

First, I explain that heated fighting creates a chemical imbalance in men that triggers an involuntary fleeing reaction. When men withdraw from conflict discussions, women become angrier, and conflict escalates. Understanding the chemistry of conflict is the first Cool-Down step.

Next, I outline the most common subjects of conflict, explain what causes conflict to turn into all-out fighting, and help you figure out whether you're suffering from out-of-control relationship warfare. I then identify the Fight Traps (dysfunctional fighting patterns) and faulty conflict-resolution tactics that heat the relationship climate and must be eliminated.

I go on to explain the way in which sexual fights result from three main factors: a man's failure to meet his partner's emotional needs, a lack of understanding of the differences between male and female sexuality, and non-sexual issues being played out in the sexual arena. And I show you how to resolve the sexual fights that stem from each of these three causes.

Then I explain that unrecognized Old Scars from childhood fuel relationship fighting. I help identify these early wounds and show how to heal them through the relationship.

After discussing the fact that distressed couples are prone to negatively distorting each other's communications, I show you how to train your mind to fight *for* you, not *against* you. Conflict resolution cannot occur until distortions are eliminated.

The last preparatory chapter provides specific Climate Control techniques that will further cool down your interactions.

The second part of the book presents my proven conflict-resolution program. I show you how to master the essential listening skills, identify and resolve nonnegotiable issues, and, finally, resolve your conflicts through the negotiation process.

I don't need to wish you good luck as you embark on this journey with me, because relationship success is not a matter of luck. It comes from learning the simple techniques described in this book and putting them into practice each day. The people I have worked with and who have followed my program are enjoying happy relationships today. Now it's your turn!

♥ ♥ ♥

Chapter One

UNDERSTANDING THE CHEMISTRY OF FIGHTING

Your husband just informed you that he's going on a white-water rafting trip with his buddies the following weekend. He smiles with boyish delight, displaying a full set of sparkling teeth, which you have to resist punching out. You have asked him, more times than you can remember, to talk with you before making plans. He forgot, clearly a case of brain flatulence. Now, you find yourself telling him, once again, how annoyed you are. Suddenly, his eyes glaze over and he turns stone deaf. He's not listening, so you turn up the heat. No use. Instead of understanding what's bugging you, he digs in his heels. This annoys you even more, so you crank up your emotional thermostat. But before you have finished, he orbits from the room and you're shouting at the back of his head.

Now you're ballistic. So you chase him to the living room, where you find him staring blindly into space, his jaw tight. You nag, whine, complain, and yell, but he ignores you.

The longer he maintains his stony silence, the more upset you become (he doesn't even love you enough to respond to your pleas). In a last-ditch effort, you push your attack to the max and hammer harder. Eureka! His silence is broken, but instead of offering words of understanding, he hurls verbal deathblows.

"Maybe you're the freakin' problem!" he shouts, swinging his fist like a club.

"Don't try to pin the blame on me! You're the one who made plans to go off."

"Who would want to spend time with a bitch?" he yells as his feet are already hitting the bricks.

The next time you try to talk to him about your issue, you're even hotter than last time. And, big surprise: he's more deaf and more defensive, or just plain "outta there" in a flash.

The preceding scenario—male retreat under fire—is also referred to as "husband withdrawal," an involuntary fleeing reaction that occurs when a man feels attacked. And according to extensive research, husband withdrawal is the number one cause of marital conflict and divorce.

Husband withdrawal is caused by a collision of two incompatible modes of handling conflict: that of the wife, who intensely expresses her hurt and anger, and that of the husband, who withdraws from the confrontation.

The technical name for this phenomenon is the *Demand/ Withdraw Negative Escalation Cycle,* and I will discuss in Chapter 7 how women can break this cycle by cooling down their emotional communications. But for now, we must concentrate on the reasons why men withdraw.

According to social science researchers J. M. Gottman and R. W. Levenson, husband withdrawal is caused by a biochemical imbalance that occurs when a man feels threatened. When this occurs, a man's autonomic nervous system (ANS) kicks into high gear. His adrenal glands begin pumping adrenaline, his heart races up to 100 beats per minute (bpm), his muscles become tense, and he is often sweating. Those are the physiological manifestations of ANS arousal; they are automatic and occur without the mediation of thought.

Men are physiologically hyperreactive to stress, a fact that has been empirically demonstrated in numerous studies. One study, by social science researchers C. W. Liberson and W. T. Liberson, yielded the finding that when men and women were faced with the same stressors, men experienced physiological disturbances, whereas women's internal chemistry remained relatively stable. Another study, by researcher L. J. P. Van Doornen, found that on an exam day, male subjects experienced biochemical imbalances, whereas females experienced no physiological changes. My own research has also demonstrated that males, but not females, experience ANS arousal during emotionally fraught discussions. The studies are clear. Men are more prone to experiencing ANS arousal in response to stress in general, and relationship conflict in particular.

When ANS arousal occurs, it triggers the fight-or-flight response, a primitive survival reaction that arises whenever a person feels emotionally or physically endangered.

3

The instinct to flee in the face of danger derives from ancient times when men were hunters and had to fight ferocious beasts. Imagine a primitive man on a mission to slay a saber-toothed tiger or rustle up some boar. He was out there facing countless threats, and his body had to be up to the task. Out jumped a tiger, and his body switched into the fight-or-flight mode, an instinctive reaction that guaranteed that he would either fight the tiger or flee for his life. This instinct was necessary to keep the hunter alive.

How does the fight-or-flight mechanism figure into the most common form of relationship conflict, the Demand/Withdraw Cycle? When a woman comes at her guy, baring her teeth, berating him with attacks and criticisms, his ANS sees danger. Modern danger does not come in the form of ferocious prey; it has evolved into the angry wife or girl-friend. And modern man is faced with the same dilemma that his primitive ancestors encountered: fight the enemy or flee.

Since a man doesn't want to assault (fight) his partner, his body sends out signals that cause him to flee, to withdraw. Withdrawal behaviors are exhibited physically, verbally, and psychically. Examples of physical fleeing include leaving the house or the room and/or avoiding contact with mate; verbal fleeing includes making excuses, justifying behavior or denying responsibility, verbal attacking, and counterblaming; and psychic fleeing, when the mind escapes, includes not listening (functional deafness), appearing stone-faced, becoming silent, or avoiding eye contact. It's important to note that all men who experience relationship distress exhibit withdrawal behaviors in one form or another.

While men are no longer hunters, their biological programming and physiological hyperreactivity to danger is still embedded in their bodies. Not aware that her man's fleeing reactions are the result of this programming, a woman becomes more and more enraged that he doesn't care about her, and unwittingly sets off more biological fire alarms in her partner. The more he withdraws, the hotter she gets, and in no time, we have chronic fighting.

To make matters worse, when ANS arousal is in high gear, it causes another physiological reaction that further intensifies conflict: a man's cognitive functions diminish, which means that reason and logic cease to exist. This brain shutoff mechanism was adaptive during prehistoric times. When primitive man was on the hunt, face-to-face with a ferocious predator, his mind was unavailable to analyze all the dangers—which was an advantage.

Is this tiger meat worth dying for? What if I fail? If I die, I'll never get laid again. . . . Maybe I don't need the meat after all. The Caveman Chronicle just ran an article about the health benefits of a vegetarian diet. I think I'll try a tofu burger tonight instead. . . . Before he could finish pondering these thoughts, he would have been hamburger meat in the beast's belly. During prehistoric times, cognitive shutdown was vital, not only for male survival, but also for the survival of the species.

Although the brain shutoff mechanism may have been a survival tool during a brief period in history, today that same mechanism may get a man "killed." When a furious woman comes at her man, the last thing he needs is a brain that's out to lunch. He needs all his higher-order cognitive functions (that is, reasoning and problem-solving skills) to handle this threat. Unfortunately, the precise tools that he needs to solve the conflict have just clicked off, and he's completely unavailable for any productive exchange. This explains why there is a great deal of patterning to the fights that occur in chronically conflicted relationships. The fights always play out in the same way, because no creative thinking is available to explore alternative fighting tactics.

Another cause of the chronicity of marital conflicts is that it takes a long time for a man's internal chemistry to normalize following stress—much longer than it does for a woman's. In fact, L. J. P. Van Doornen's research has shown that in relationships in which conflict is frequent, a man's chemistry never returns to baseline. With each subsequent fight, his arousal mounts higher and higher, and his fuse becomes shorter and shorter, placing him at risk of acting out physically before he has a chance to flee. This risk is especially great for impulsive men who are already prone to physically acting out. (It should be noted here that domestic violence is not the focus of this book. And if a woman is involved with a man who batters, or if she feels physically endangered, she is advised to seek professional help.)

The point to keep in mind is that in all chronically conflicted relationships, residual ANS arousal and chronic cognitive shutdown fuel ongoing discord.

> *George returned home, and without his knowing it, a common fight was brewing.*
> *"Did you buy the milk?" his wife, Mary, asked.*
> *"No. I forgot," he answered, blank-faced.*
> *"I reminded you to stop on your way home!" Mary scolded.*
> *George stared at her, speechless.*
> *"You aren't hearing a word I'm saying!"*
> *"Yes, I am!"*
> *"What did I say?"*
> *George stared at her, his jaw clenched.*

"I'll refresh your memory. You said you forgot to get the milk!"

"I know!"

"So. What about the six-pack you're carrying?"

"Well . . . I bought it at the gas station," George said, closing his eyes.

"Since when did they stop selling milk at the gas station?"

"I can't remember everything. You don't care how hard my day was." He turned away.

"What's that got to do with the milk? As always, you forgot because what I want isn't important."

"That's not true. I buy you things," he said, still looking away.

"What?" Mary asked, raising her voice.

"Well, cookies, ice cream, pizza!" he shouted.

"And you eat them yourself. I'm tired of listening to your excuses. Admit it . . . you forgot the friggin' milk!"

"Yes, I forgot your freakin' milk. I have other more important things to think about, like how to survive life with a witch." George stormed out and slammed the door.

In this example, George demonstrates a serious case of brain meltdown due to chronic ANS arousal. Cognitive shutdown also caused George's *inability* to process communications, signaled by closing the eyes and/or looking away. Apart from becoming a mental midget, what else is happening to poor George? The muscles throughout his body are rigid, hence that blank, frozen stare that his wife interprets as his not caring about her. And his muscles are tensed in preparation for fight or flight. Since George loves his wife, he does not want to fight her, so he flees instead.

The first form of fleeing George engaged in was psychic withdrawal. His mind escaped the scene; he tuned out, appeared deaf, and avoided eye contact. Mary became outraged by his seeming lack of caring, and she cranked up the heat. George's ANS arousal mounted, and he slipped into verbal fleeing—hurling excuses, being defensive, denying, and refusing to accept responsibility for his upsetting behavior. The verbal fleeing further infuriated Mary ("How dare he turn the tables on me?"), and she became more aggressive, which intensified George's ANS arousal.

Since verbal fleeing didn't succeed in defusing the situation, George's body physically fled. He escaped from the room in order to reestablish his chemical equilibrium. But unfortunately, in this altercation and every other time George physically withdraws, Mary interprets his behavior as further proof of his lack of caring. She becomes angrier and angrier; George's ANS arousal mounts higher and higher, so that he is constantly receiving internal signals to flee from danger. And what's worse, these distress signals become part of his "normal" state of functioning. Constant ANS arousal causes chronic cognitive shutdown, which explains why George habitually forgets the milk. So long as George's chemistry remains disturbed, he will continue to withdraw. Mary, in turn, will continue to be angry, which ensures the continuance of George's disturbed chemistry, and their chronic fighting is the result.

Is Disturbed Body Chemistry (ANS Arousal) Causing Your Fighting?

A True/False Test for Women	
Our fights seem scripted. Our words, gestures, or actions rarely vary.	T or F
I can predict the outcome of our fights ahead of time.	T or F
When we fight, he seems to be frozen like a statue.	T or F
If I were to take his pulse, it would be racing (100 bpm or greater) during a fight.	T or F
My partner sweats during a fight.	T or F
My partner's muscles are very tight during a fight.	T or F
My partner turns away from me during a fight.	T or F
My partner closes his eyes and won't make eye contact with me during a fight.	T or F
My partner has a blank, frozen stare during a fight.	T or F
My partner defends, justifies, or counterblames during a fight.	T or F
My partner doesn't seem to be listening to me during a fight.	T or F
My partner physically leaves to escape a fight in progress.	T or F
My partner avoids me when he thinks a fight is brewing.	T or F

If you answered *true* to any of the above, we have a fairly clear idea that your partner's withdrawal and your chronic fights are caused by disturbed body chemistry. Why am I bothering to give you a chemistry lesson? Because the first step to preventing the number one cause of relationship conflict and divorce starts with understanding that your husband's, lover's, or boyfriend's various withdrawal behaviors are not a sign of lack of love. They spring from a primitive, biologically based mechanism that he cannot help.

If this is the way men are wired, what can be done about it? Read on. In the following chapters, I will outline all the factors that heat the marital climate and discuss how to modify them. Until the thermostat is turned down, no conflict resolution can occur.

Chapter Two

THE RELATIONSHIP BATTLEGROUND:

Identifying and Rating Your Conflicts on the Fighting Richter Scale

Sue and Henry are standing in the bathroom, embroiled in what might be called a plumbing power struggle. Henry always leaves the toilet seat up in the middle of the night. Sue invariably falls in the bowl and receives an unwanted buttocks bath. Standing in the bathroom, her butt dripping wet, she begins to wonder if another living soul can identify with the heartbreak of chapped cheeks.

If Sue had access to a library database, she could research the question. And, perhaps more important, she could determine if a judge would consider dishpan buns as grounds for divorce. Strange as it may seem, many divorces have occurred over such seemingly trivial conflicts.

In this chapter, I'll be discussing relationship conflict—the most common subjects of conflict and what causes conflict to turn into all-out fighting—and I'll help you figure out whether you are suffering from out-of-control relationship warfare.

Before we go further, however, let's make sure you are clear on what constitutes "conflict." Conflict is a clash that occurs whenever opposing needs, wishes, goals, or opinions arise in a relationship. Since marriage and other intimate relationships are made up of two separate individuals, conflict and the angry feelings that go with it are normal and to be expected, according to researcher S. Duck.

Conflict Causes

What are the most common subjects of conflict? As you read over the following list, keep in mind that it's simply a quick overview and by no means definitive. You also need to know that complaints are generally issued by women—hence the fact that the complainer in the following examples is usually female.

Affection Conflicts

Disagreement over the frequency of affection displays (hugging, kissing, saying kind words, romantic gestures, and the like). One spouse desires more emotional displays than the other is willing to give.

> *"The last time you kissed me was when we said, 'I do'!"*
> *"You pet that dog more than me!"*
> *"Do you think it would kill you to say something nice to me once before I die?"*
> *"You're as romantic as a stuffed doll!"*

Where's the Beef?

Otherwise known as sexual conflicts—conflicts over manner, frequency, technique, and so on. These are the arguments over "when," "where," "how," "how much," and "how long" (no, I'm not referring to measurements, although that could be a source of conflict as well).

> *"You're about as gentle as a buzz saw!"*
> *"You think you might get in the mood before the century ends?"*

Intimacy Issues

Disagreements regarding the degree of emotional and physical closeness or distance in the relationship. One partner wants more time apart than the other. One person never listens to the other's feelings or spends too little time at home. One partner never communicates his/her own inner feelings to the other.

> *"You're always out with your friends or working!"*
> *"You never spend any time with me and the kids!"*

Leisure Arguments

Disagreements over how much time should be spent on leisure activities. Disagreements over what types of activities should be performed and whether these pursuits should be conducted separately or together.

"My idea of a good Sunday is not refilling beer pitchers for you and your friends!"
"Do you think that we could do something together for a change?"

Jealousy Arguments

Whenever one partner pays attention to someone else, the other becomes insanely jealous. The jealous partner often thinks that the other is flirting with someone else (even when this is not true).

"Maybe you'd rather go home with her [or him]?"
"Why didn't you announce to everyone that you had the hots for him [or her]?"
"I saw you holding her shoulder and caressing her neck!"
"You said you would be in your office until seven. I called you at six-thirty. There was no answer. Where were you?"

Household-Chore Arguments

Disagreements over the perceived lack of fairness in the division of chores arising from one partner's feeling stuck with a disproportionate share of the responsibilities or from one partner's refusal to assist around the house.

"Where is it written that I'm the only one who should wash the dishes [or do the laundry, etc.]?"
"How many times do I have to tell you to pick up your papers from the friggin' counter?"

Lack-of-Follow-Through Arguments

In these arguments, it's generally the woman who is angry at her partner for not following through with his agreed-upon tasks.

"You forgot to take the garbage out <u>again!</u>"
"It was your turn to pick up Johnny from soccer. Where were you?"

Lack-of-Initiative Arguments

Types of arguments in which one partner is angry that the other doesn't even notice, or seem to care, that various tasks require attention.

"How many months are you going to wait before you fix the broken kitchen window?"
"When were you going to notice that Sally's bike has a flat tire? It's been four months!"

Parenting Arguments

Disagreement over the degree of lenience or strictness; feeling that one partner undermines the other, doesn't enforce the rules that have been agreed upon, or reverses the decisions of the other parent. Feelings of resentment over unequal distribution of child-care responsibilities.

"You're like one of the kids. You let them do whatever they want!"
"What are you, an army sergeant?"
"Why should I bother making rules when you just let the kids break them?"
"This fabric that I'm holding in my hand is called a diaper. Do you think it would kill you to change one every now and then?"

In-Law Arguments

Fights over loyalty issues, such as feeling sided-against in a family argument. Disagreements on how much time should be spent with the in-laws.

"Why don't you marry your mother?"
"You always take their side over mine!"
"Since you want to see your folks so much, why don't we just move in with them?"

Friendship Arguments

Disagreements over choice of friends, how much time should be spent socializing with friends in the absence of the other partner, how much time should be spent socializing with friends or other couples.

> *"Why did you marry me? You obviously like being with your buddies more than with me!"*
>
> *"I don't like your friend Walter. He always puts me down. Why do we have to spend time with him?"*

Value Conflicts

Disagreements over life goals; what is important in life; cultural, religious, or sexual values; drinking or smoking habits; not seeing eye to eye on tastes or interests, which includes conflicts over what is proper behavior in social situations.

> *"Now I know why you call your Land Rover a 'pickup' truck! And no, I'm not interested in using your backseat as my box spring."*
>
> *"You make Ben Franklin look like a big spender!"*
>
> *"You shouldn't drink on Sunday!"*
>
> *"You don't go to church enough!"*
>
> *"Why do we need to redecorate so often?"*

Selfishness or Lack-of-Cooperation Arguments

An unwillingness to work with the partner toward a mutually satisfying resolution of whatever the conflict is. One partner feels that the other is persistently stubborn or unresponsive.

> *"You don't give a damn how I feel!"*
>
> *"You don't care about what I want!"*

Control Arguments

In these arguments, one of the partners feels controlled or manipulated by the other. A partner or spouse who needs to be in charge is often frightened of being controlled. Thus, the person who rules others does so in order to prevent him- or herself from being taken over.

> *"Why does it always have to be your way?"*
> *"You're not my father."*

Money Arguments

Disagreements over bills, how much money should be allocated to savings versus how much should be spent outright. Disagreements over one partner's overspending, stinginess, or overly controlling stance with regard to money.

> *"You're as tight as a frog's butt!"*
> *"You spend money like water!"*
> *"There's always money to buy your new computer, your printer, your software programs, even your computer games. For me, though, it's never in the budget. I haven't bought a dress in the last three years."*

Power-Struggle Arguments

Squabbles over any issue that you can imagine, and neither partner is willing to yield. There are no compromises, and the mates soon feel like dogs fighting over the same bone. The movie *The War of the Roses* depicts a power struggle that ends in death. Remember that even if one partner succeeds in prevailing, both partners are losers when power struggles have taken over the relationship.

"You always need to have it your way!"
"I'd die before I'd give in to you."

You're-Shutting-Me-Out Arguments

Arguments in which it's usually the woman who complains that her partner doesn't disclose his thoughts and feelings to her.

"You never let me in."
"I know something is bothering you. Why won't you talk to me?"

You-Never-Listen-to-Me Arguments

This is a common relationship beef. And, once again, it's the woman who usually complains about not being emotionally heard.

"Why can't you just listen to what I'm saying?"
"Don't walk away from me when I'm talking."

Whatever you're chronically fighting about probably fits into one of the above categories. Interestingly, these sources of conflict are not only remarkably consistent from nation to nation, but with the exception of the You-Never-Listen-to-Me argument, they occur among happy couples as well. *So, you ask, why are they happy while I'm so <u>unhappy?</u>* The reason is simple. Studies have shown that while happy couples fight about exactly the same things that unhappy couples do, happy couples do not fight *habitually* on these subjects. They have acquired the interactional tools that permit them to resolve their conflicts, whereas unhappy couples employ ineffective conflict-resolution techniques so that their disagreements cycle out of control long before they can ever reach the resolution stage. That is, their fighting becomes so heated that the man withdraws and no resolution occurs.

In the next chapter, I'll help you identify the various behaviors that are causing your conflicts to cycle out of control. In later chapters, I'll show you how to apply more effective techniques so that you can pull in the reins long before your conflicts become runaway horses.

Conflict vs. Fighting

It is necessary to make the distinction between *conflict* and *fighting.* The words are often used interchangeably, despite the fact that they are different. Whenever our needs and wishes are thwarted, a state of conflict results. If the conflict is not resolved amicably, anger arises. It is how we handle the anger that determines whether or not a conflict will become a fight.

Most unhappy couples do not know how to channel angry feelings into constructive communications. Instead, they think that angry feelings are synonymous with angry actions, and they "act out" their anger. The distinction between the feeling and the acting out is essential because anger is a neutral emotion, a warning light that your psychological toes have been stepped on. The acting out of anger through hostile behavior (door slamming, shoving, and the like) or hostile words (name-calling, sarcasm, threats, insults) is a big problem. Hostile words and actions evolve into fighting. You may say to me, "My relationship problems are driving me crazy, and if I couldn't blow off steam, I'd lose it for sure." While you may feel better at the moment you drop your load, what you probably don't realize is that the ranting, raving, screaming, yelling, and slamming actually cause more problems.

There was an era when therapists touted the benefits of emotional "venting." A branch of psychology known as the *cathartic school* propagated the notion that it's healthy to scream and yell in order to reach to the bottom of one's emotional barrel—kind of like an enema for the soul. This approach to handling emotions has been largely abandoned because, as it turns out, anger has a self-feeding aspect: anger begets more anger. In addition, emotional venting has a negative effect on the partner who is being dumped on. I have already explained in Chapter 1 why acting out of intense emotions triggers a chemical reaction in men that actually causes more marital conflict. But for now, let's just focus on the point that raw emotion should never be dumped on a mate—that is, not if you want to resolve your conflicts and achieve relationship harmony.

If acting out anger doesn't work, what about expressing angry feelings in words? Now I'm really going to throw you a curveball by saying that angry feelings should never be "expressed." What I mean is that raw, angry emotions should never be delivered in pure form to your mate. I find it helpful to use the image of a sieve when talking about intense, angry feelings. Before discussing with your mate what is bothering you, your raw emotions need to be filtered through this imaginary sieve. What remains in the sieve is to be kept for yourself, and only what passes through the sieve of your intellect is fit for human consumption. The important point here is that once the emotions have passed through this sieve, they have been transformed and detoxified.

Roger was a 30-year-old copy editor at a daily newspaper. He chain-smoked while ranting about the lousy copy that the reporters turn in, and at home, he ruled his family with an iron fist. When his kids strayed from what he has decided is the right path, he barraged them with fits of rage. And if his wife, Jane, a sexy bleached blonde, dared to smile at another man at a party, she received a verbal lashing during the ride home. After years of suffering these painful explosions, Jane bared her soul to her minister, who referred her to me.

I met with Roger, who explained that his wife and kids made him so furious that he could not control his behavior—the mesh of his emotional sieve was as widely spaced as the San Andreas Fault. I inquired about other situations in which Roger expressed powerful rage.

"What about your boss? Doesn't he make you angry at times?" I asked.

"Yeah, he pisses me off all the time," Roger admitted.

"And how many times have you given it to him?"

Roger blinked a couple of times, obviously thinking, *This shrink I got is really off her rocker.* "Yell at him? Are you nuts, doc? I need my job. You think I'm crazy?"

So, Roger had the ability to control himself when he wanted to. He had an emotional sieve with a very fine mesh at his disposal. That is, when Roger realized that his opponent had more power than he did—the power to fire him, as in the case of his boss—then he could be a good boy.

"If you are able to control your behavior when you are enraged at a boss whom you hate, then you can control yourself when dealing with your wife and kids whom you love," I said.

Roger was speechless. I advised him to join one of my therapy groups for impulsive behavior. After a few months of regular attendance, Roger had decided to use the same sieve with his wife and kids that had proved so effective in filtering his emotions when his boss enraged him. He had put his emotions under his control.

It is essential that you learn to harness your raw emotions and transform them into constructive communications that are helpful to you, your mate, and your relationship. The key here is this: how anger is handled makes or breaks a relationship. Remember as you read on that it's acted-out anger that causes occasional relationship conflicts to turn into out-of-control fighting.

Fight Habituation

For some couples, out-of-control fighting is precisely what they unconsciously want to maintain. No matter how uncomfortable their fighting may be, the prospect of *not* fighting may be even more uncomfortable. For example, chronic fighting may ward off other feelings that may be too terrifying to one or both of the mates. Being hooked on fighting is what psychologists call "fight habituation."

Mark and Joan are a classic example of what I call Fighting Junkies. Mark is terrified of intimacy, and whenever they seem to be getting along better, he does something to make Joan angry. For example, he gets a speeding ticket, which depletes their savings, and the fighting that ensues serves to keep Joan at a comfortable distance. No matter how hard they try to change, they always end up fighting again.

As with any addiction, trying to kick the habit can make you feel sicker before you feel better. How can you tell if you're hooked on fighting? Take this simple test.

Are You a Fighting Junkie?	
I secretly look for things to fight about.	T or F
I feel most comfortable when at war.	T or F
I go for the kill when we're fighting, saying and doing things that I know will push my mate's buttons.	T or F
I don't want to let my partner close to me; I'm afraid he would hurt or reject me.	T or F
My mother and father used to fight all the time when I was a kid.	T or F
We have been fighting ever since our relationship began, even when we were dating.	T or F

If you answered *true* to any of the above questions, you may be a Fighting Junkie, and you will need to pay extra attention to Chapter 5: Battle Scars, which will help get you beyond your addiction.

Out-of-control fighting is not always caused by an unconscious need to ward off closeness. It may also result from a deficit in conflict-resolution skills. Without these skills, fighting becomes a runaway horse, and once it has taken off, the horse is very hard to get back in the stable. And there's more: What is true of one single fighting episode is also true of the life sequence of relationship fights. Multiple unresolved conflicts follow a downward spiral that is not unlike a chronic health condition. Left untreated, a physical illness usually worsens, whereas if you catch it early enough and intervene properly, you're likely to cure the problem. The same is true for an intimate relationship. It's a living, breathing entity, and if you abuse it and ignore its signs of sickness, it will die.

The first step toward a cure and toward gaining control is to determine the severity of your fighting.

Rate Your Conflicts on the Fighting Richter Scale

The following stages are the three main gradations on the Richter Scale, Stage 3 being the most advanced.

Stage 1: The Broken Record

The first sign that fighting is out of control is technically referred to as Stability of Conflict, or what I call the Broken Record phenomenon. Do you find yourself bringing up the same issues over and over again? No matter how trivial the subjects of conflict may seem, if you are regularly clashing on the same issues, you're in big trouble. What does the Broken Record phenomenon look like?

"I hate it when you walk around the house in your bra and panties—with the shades open. How many times have I asked you not to do it? A hundred,

two hundred, five hundred times? Each time you say okay, but two days later, you do it again. Here's the phone—why don't you just call the neighbor and tell him you're ready to sleep with him?"

"This morning, for the six hundredth time, you didn't put the cap on the toothpaste tube. I'm fed up with you!"

"I've asked you to avoid making long calls to your mother that use up all the minutes on our cell-phone plan. I asked you last year, last month, last week, and even two days ago. But you do it again and again. Why don't you move to Florida with her?"

If you find yourself arguing recycled issues, no doubt about it, you're stuck in Stage 1. You need to learn the conflict-resolution skills presented in this book or you will soon slip into Stage 2.

Stage 2: Withdrawal

Stage 2 emerges when your areas of conflict have become major hot spots. This stage is like the old French proverb: *Cats that have been burned by hot water become afraid of cold water.* In other words, all you have to do is bring up the recycled issue, and your partner's fur is already bristling.

For example, Marjorie's husband goes bowling too many nights a week. For months she complained more and more about it, while he sat there listening to her tirades. Eventually, he turned a deaf ear. Now all she has to do is open her mouth to speak, and the bowling ball is in his hand and he's rolling out the door.

In Stage 2, a man has begun to withdraw physically, emotionally, or psychically whenever a conflict discussion arises or whenever he thinks one is brewing. The following list gives you, in more detail than the previous chapter, the classic signs of male withdrawal:

- When you try to talk to your partner about what's bothering you, he stares off into space and has a blank expression.

- He turns away from you or avoids eye contact when you try to speak.

- He becomes sullen and silent, and appears not to be listening.

- He defends himself in words, hurls all kinds of excuses, and denies whatever is the issue on the table. Or he tries to counterattack by telling you what you've done wrong since day one.

- He physically leaves the room or the house.

- He spends as much time as possible away from home, hides out in his study or his workshop, or disappears by watching television for hours.

If you find that your partner is exhibiting any of these behaviors, you two are locked in the Demand/Withdraw Negative Escalation Cycle, and if you don't start applying the principles in this book (and pay particular attention to cooling down the relationship climate), statistics show that you will likely be separated or divorced within three years.

Stage 3: The Bitter End

In this stage, you are so tired of fighting that you've begun to give up. You may have stopped bringing up the troublesome issues because you're in the process of detaching psychologically. Maybe you're fantasizing about having an affair; or you're making plans for your future, and the plans don't include your partner. This is a process that's similar to coming to terms with the death of a loved one. First there is anger, then there is detachment, and finally acceptance. In this stage, you are trying to convince yourself that you don't care anymore so that the leaving won't be so painful. When relationship distress has reached this level, if you're asked to remember the good times you've shared as a couple, your memory will draw a blank. It's as if your mind has pulled its own plug so that your heart won't suffer too much when you dissolve the relationship.

Ben and Josephine have been together for 14 years. He owns an auto-repair shop. She's a hairdresser. Josephine has often asked Ben to tell her when he'll be home. She begged, she cried, she screamed. He continued to come home when he pleased, often past ten o'clock, only to throw himself in bed, snoring almost before his head hit the pillow.

"Hi, how are you?" he mumbled one night, stumbling half-drunk into the bedroom.

"Okay," she called from the bathroom while preparing to meet her friend at the local hangout. She put on her coat and walked to the front door. "Good night," she said flatly before closing the door.

If Ben and Josephine don't apply my techniques quickly, they will soon become a divorce statistic.

Even if you are in Stage 3, don't despair. The techniques that you will soon learn have helped other desperate couples, even those on the verge of signing divorce papers, rekindle the love they thought was long lost. But before you can resolve the conflicts that have transformed your relationship into a cold war, your hearts must thaw.

If you are suffering from chronic fighting and find yourself caught in any of the three stages mentioned above, the next thing you must do is identify and eradicate the Fight Traps and faulty conflict-resolution tactics that stand between you and relationship harmony.

♥ ♥ ♥

Chapter Three

THE NO-FLY (OFF THE HANDLE) ZONE:

Eliminating Fight Traps and Faulty Conflict-Resolution Tactics

Each of the Fight Traps and faulty conflict-resolution tactics discussed in this chapter throws oil on the fire and keeps couples stuck on the fighting treadmill. If you want to achieve relationship harmony, you must ditch them all. Before we get down to identifying your Fight Traps and faulty conflict-resolution tactics, we first need to find out if you are truly ready to give them up.

Every night after work, Fred practices the same ritual without deviation. He deposits his shoes at the back door, nestles into his favorite easy chair, pours himself a scotch, browses through the paper, and dozes.

We humans are creatures of habit, yet there is a permanent tug-of-war going on inside all of us, however hidden it may be. On one level we want to move ahead, and on another we want to stay the same. Take the following test.

If I am honest with myself, I have to admit that I'd feel like a fish out of water without our chronic fights gnawing at the guts of our relationship.	T or F
I am afraid we wouldn't know how to relate to each other if we stopped our fighting.	T or F
I am afraid that if we let go of our fighting, another worse problem will appear.	T or F
I am afraid that if I allow myself to believe that things can change for the better, I'll be terribly disappointed if it doesn't happen.	T or F

If you said *true* to the first or second statement, you're suffering from fear of the unknown. This is a normal fear.

Each night, Jennifer made sure that Joseph's dinner was ready at 6:30. Joseph, an accountant, told her that he'd be arriving later and later each night as the tax deadline approached. When this started happening, Jennifer was convinced that he was using the taxes as a pretext for avoiding her. So when he finally arrived home, she lashed out at him. He silently tolerated each verbal attack—eventually she'd run out of gas, and there would be peace until the next time. For him, being yelled at was part of marriage; his mother always screamed at his father. At least there were no surprises.

One day, Jennifer complained to her friend Susan about her problem with Joseph. Susan, whose father was also an accountant, told Jennifer that her father stayed out until 11 P.M. during tax season. Jennifer realized that she was misinterpreting Joseph's lateness.

When he returned home that night, she didn't scream at him, but welcomed him with a kiss and a big hello. Joseph felt frightened. *What's going on? Has Jennifer poisoned my stew? What does she want from me? Maybe she's horny and wants to coerce me into having sex. . . . Not another hour and a half to stay awake . . . and on a night when I'm so tired.* Joseph began sweating. His guts were in a knot. He had become so accustomed to their nightly fight that he hardly knew how to live without it. He was suffering from fear of the unknown.

True, the unknown can be scary. But chronic fighting is even scarier. What do you risk by staying with the familiar? Possibilities include physical violence, illness, depression, infidelity, and divorce. Write down all the risks you face from staying the same.

As you ponder all the terrible risks associated with staying stuck on the fighting treadmill, aren't you more willing to take a chance on the new?

What about the last two statements, "If we let go of our fighting, another worse problem will appear" and "If I allow myself to believe that things can change for the better, I'll be terribly disappointed if it doesn't happen"? Both fears express a defeatist attitude. It's like saying, "I know I'm doomed, so why try for better?" This hopeless feeling may be coming from the fact that you haven't been able to make headway on your relationship problems. It's normal to feel defeated when things aren't going well. But by the time you finish reading this book, you will have proven techniques to use to combat this attitude.

There is also a deeper meaning behind this defeatist attitude. Your mind is using this hopeless philosophy as a protection against feeling hurt or disappointed. If you try and fail, of course you will feel let down. So, in order to protect yourself, your mind has convinced you not to try. (*Why bother—it won't work anyway.*) True, if you don't expend effort in attempting to change the situation, then you don't have to risk failure, hurt, or disappointment. But the irony is that by not trying, you are failing yourself and your relationship. Remember, the only real failures are those who don't try. Identifying the fears that keep you clinging to the familiar is the first step toward resolving them. I also suggest that you frequently reread the three paragraphs above, which will help further soften your fears. When your fears no longer have you by the throat, you're ready to move on to the next step: to identify and eliminate the Fight Traps that are holding your relationship hostage.

Discovering Your Fight Traps

In the last 30 years, I have worked with many couples from all walks of life, and this work has yielded a fascinating finding: Fight Traps cut across state lines, class lines, power lines, age lines, and any other kind of lines you can think of. That is to say, all conflicted couples engage in them.

When I conducted research for this book, I searched the literature and was surprised that I could not find a comprehensive list of Fight Traps. So what you're about to read is the first exhaustive list, which I have broken down into two categories: *Open Warfare* and *Secret Warfare.*

It's important that you realize that every trap is faulty. I am stressing this point because most of us engage in behaviors that are so natural that they seem like a second skin. No matter how "normal" these Fight Traps may seem to you, remember that they are neither normal nor healthy. Each and every one of them maintains and escalates relationship conflict and keeps you stuck in a permanent state of war. So, if you're committed to achieving marital harmony, it's vital to identify the Fight Traps you and your mate use and trash them.

Fight Traps: Open Warfare

Counterblaming

In distressed relationships, couples rarely listen to their partners and will miss no opportunity to throw the blame back on each other. Counterblaming escalates conflict and precludes resolution.

> *Mary:* I asked you not to leave your underwear beside the bed.
> *Pete:* I told you not to hang your stockings in the shower.
> *Mary:* You always have an answer, Mr. Perfect.
> *Pete:* You're the one who's answering back.

Verbal Attacking

As you'll see in the following example, Verbal Attacking leads to defensive responses and verbal counterattacks.

> *Marie is standing in the laundry room, the blue vein in her temple beating faster than a jackhammer. As Josh enters the room, she hurls a wet towel at his head, and it coils like a turban around his skull.*
> *"You seem to be clueless to the fact that laundry needs to be done each week," she snarls.*
> *"Oh, like I do nothing around the house [defensive]. Not that you would notice [counterattack]," he shouts, peeling the towel from his head.*

Scorekeeping

Couples get caught in scorekeeping to boost their eroding egos, and we'll talk about this in greater depth in Chapter 6. For now, I simply want to show you how to recognize scorekeeping and its variants. Keep in mind that once a couple resorts to this Fight Trap, they will use any ammunition necessary in order to win. Consequently, it's not unusual to find that all the tactics described in this section may be creatively combined in order to strengthen the punch.

> *Mike:* This is the fifth time that I told you to fold my socks flat and not in a ball.
> *Sue:* Well, as long as we're counting, it's been a hundred times that I told you to stop piling your junk mail on your night table.

Mike: If you're gonna try to paint me as the pig, I think you'd better look at your closet. It's got a thousand pieces of junk thrown in there!

Sue: Since you're so good with numbers, here's the phone. Dial up your mother and tell her you're moving back in with her.

Winners/Losers

With this Fight Trap, one member of the couple focuses on winning and making the other a loser.

Elaine: You forgot to pick up my car part.

Rick: I'm sorry.

Elaine: I can't rely on you.

Rick: I said I was sorry. You won't be satisfied until you grind me into the dirt.

Elaine: That's where you belong!

I'm Right, You're Wrong

I'm Right, You're Wrong is characterized by one member of the couple focusing on winning the argument and proving the other wrong.

Fred: You shouldn't face the net when you're hitting a backhand shot.

Sarah: I'm married to Andy friggin' Murray!

Fred: I'm just telling you how to improve your shot. You know I'm a better player than you are.

Sarah: Yes, you're right. You're a better player and a better chef and a better expert in everything.

Fred: What are you talking about? I never pretended to be a laundry expert!

Character Assassination

Character Assassination includes name-calling, insults, and put-downs.

> *Steve:* You know, you are a real loser!
> *Louise:* You should talk. You're lazy as hell!
> *Steve:* I'm not the gutless one who won't dare ask for a raise.

Globalizing

With this Fight Trap, broad generalizations are made, and statements that include the phrases "you always" and "you never" are common.

> *Brenda:* You know you never take me on dates anymore.
> *Scott:* You're always nagging me. Why would I want to?

Kitchen-Sinking

When couples are in the throes of Kitchen-Sinking, they throw everything that's bothering them into one discussion.

> *Rose:* I'm pretty fed up with your falling asleep on the couch.
> *Rich:* I'm tired.

Rose: You're tired? You never have time to spend with the kids. You never talk to me anymore. There's no romance.

Rich: Anything else?

Rose: Yeah, and you don't make enough money.

Throwing Oil on the Fire

When couples use this Fight Trap, they make inflammatory comments that they know will anger the other person. This trap is popularly referred to as Pushing Someone's Buttons.

Suzie: I have a good mind to call my old boyfriend and ask him to take me out.

Robert: You know how it drives me crazy when you get back at me by trying to make me jealous.

Fighting Dirty or Hitting Below the Belt

In this Fight Trap, the angry person will use out-of-context information to deliver a low blow. For example, let's say a wife reveals to her mate that she's upset because her boss said that her work isn't well organized. Then, a few days later, she tells her husband that he's being too messy around the house. The hitting-below-the-belt fighter would get even by saying something like, "Who are you to talk? I thought you won the Miss Piggy Award at the office."

Ancient History

Bringing up something that the other said or did in the recent or remote past is what I call the Ancient History Fight Trap.

Emily: Here we go again. You're looking at that woman with lust. Just like you did with the blonde last week.

Eric: I am not.

Emily: You sure are. You've been doing this since the first day of our marriage. Remember when we were sitting at the bar on our honeymoon?

Exploding

When angered, the exploder gets out of control—screams, rants, raves, and may even become verbally or physically abusive. This behavior has two effects on the receiving partner: he or she either becomes a doormat or attacks back. In the latter case, physical violence often results. Professional help is needed when explosive behavior is present.

Power Plays

This tactic is used by a person who possesses power over his or her partner. Power can be in the form of money, better looks, or even the knowledge that the other partner is so in love or dependent that he or she would put up with garbage rather than risk losing the relationship. When someone misuses power, he or she is the boss and there is no discussion or collaboration. The partner who wields the power is generally quite happy with this approach because it yields what he or she wants. But watch out—the crushed partner is probably doing a slow burn and waiting for the chance to pay back the powerful partner in spades.

The following are good examples of how misuse of power sounds:

> *"I said our daughter is not going on that trip, and that's the end of it. Period."*
> *"This discussion is terminated."*
> *"My answer is final."*

One-Upmanship

In the One-Upmanship Fight Trap, one partner is bent on proving that his or her issue or problem is bigger and more important than the other's.

> *Bob:* You think you've got something to cry about? I've got more stress on me in an ordinary day of work than you have in a month.
> *Bridgette:* Poor you. You've got it so tough. Who do you think got up last night to take care of Suzy?

Recruiting Allies

Recruiting Allies refers to the practice of getting outsiders or family members to take sides.

> *Sharon:* My mother even told me that you're wrong not to pay for my new dress.
> *Tom:* Why doesn't she pay for it?

Sharon: She's not my husband. She said that if you were a good husband, you'd pay for it.

Tom: The guys at work think I should buy a cheaper wife!

Fight Traps: Secret Warfare

In Secret Warfare, partners still escalate conflicts; they just do so in subtler, less overt ways. Keep in mind that Secret Warfare nevertheless fuels ongoing fighting.

Guilt Trip

The partner who engages in the Guilt Trip Fight Trap literally blames the other partner for anything and everything.

Guilt Tripper: I hope you're satisfied. You got me so upset over your temper outburst that I have a terrible headache.

Silent Treatment

With the Silent Treatment Fight Trap, one partner punishes the other with silence.

Steve: How long are you going to ignore me? Marie walks away, as though deaf.

Withholding

In order to express his or her anger, the withholder, consciously or unconsciously, doesn't provide whatever it is the other person wants.

"I get it. No sex for me until I buy you flowers."

or

Ethel: Did you remember we have a date tonight?
Scott: I just forgot.
Ethel: You always "forget" when I made you mad the night before!

Silent Sabotage

This is a combination of Silent Treatment and Withholding. The person doesn't verbally express anger, but rather gets even silently or indirectly.

Monty: You keep burning my dinner.
Gabrielle: I don't know what you mean.
Monty: You've been mad at me all week. You burned dinner three times, and you also wrecked three of my shirts.

I Told You So

With this Fight Trap, one partner makes a point of rubbing the other partner's nose in his or her mistakes.

43

Karl: The toilet's broken again!

Betty: I told you not to use that plumber. You should have listened to me!

Sarcasm

In distressed relationships, this Fight Trap often takes the form of a statement that communicates agreement that isn't truly sincere.

Bud (smirking): Yes, you're right.

Natalie: Don't "yes" me. You know you don't mean it.

Bud: Oh, but I do mean it. Every husband wants his wife to take a $25,000 trip across the globe with her sisters.

Ambusher

The Ambusher is a person who hides, waiting to launch a surprise attack or to prey upon the spouse when he or she is weakest.

"I can't believe you choose this moment—when I'm upset—to complain about my lovemaking techniques."

Indirect Digs

In this trap, one partner doesn't directly tell the other what he or she is angry about, but waits until they're in public, then drops snide remarks.

Sue and Mike are out to dinner with friends. The night before, Mike rushed foreplay, but Sue didn't say anything at the time. As the group waits for their table, Sue's friend says, "I'm so hungry, I can hardly wait."

To which Sue replies, in a loud voice, "You're not the only one. My husband can't wait, either."

Nagging, Whining, and Complaining: The Three Scrooges

Women are particularly inclined to express anger indirectly by resorting to these three self-explanatory behaviors. They are especially dangerous Fight Traps because they always provoke husband withdrawal.

Faulty Conflict-Resolution Tactics

Now that we have discussed the various Fight Traps, let's identify a few more potholes on the path to relationship harmony. Conflict-resolution impasses can be due to universal obstacles, couple type, and individual obstacles—the faulty conflict-resolution tactics of one or both partners.

Universal Obstacles to Conflict Resolution

The primary universal obstacle to resolution is ANS arousal. So when your partner seems unwilling to work with you, check his pulse or his pits; if his Safeguard has stopped working, you know ANS arousal has kicked in. And if ANS arousal is in full swing, you must wait to discuss matters. No man can sit for a conflict discussion until his arousal level has diminished.

Old Scars

When I speak of Old Scars, I'm referring to the wounds that still linger from childhood. I will devote an entire chapter to this topic, but for now, I just want you to become aware that Old Scars are another universal obstacle to conflict resolution and that they interfere with conflict resolution in two ways.

First, when a woman's Old Scars are activated by her partner's behavior, she will become very emotionally upset, which will trigger ANS arousal in her partner. Likewise, a man's unresolved Old Scars are likely to interfere with his ability to negotiate with his partner. This, in turn, will anger her and trigger his ANS arousal. In Chapter 5, I discuss Old Scars fully, and I will help you determine whether they are fueling your fights and interfering with your negotiation potential. The point to remember now is this: you will need to provide each other with the necessary emotional healing as a precondition to resolving your conflicts.

The Seesaw Effect

If ANS arousal and Old Scars are not causing your mate's refusal to collaborate or negotiate, there's a good chance that the Seesaw Effect is operating. It is believed that when there is love, a man will move mountains to keep that love. But no matter how much a man loves you, love and power are hinged together much like a seesaw. When power is on the upswing, the willingness to collaborate is often on the downswing. This leads to what I call the Male Power Play.

Male Power Play: Refusal to Negotiate

Many women are bereft of power in their relationships. They either don't earn as much as their spouses or don't earn at all. In many cases, women need their partners for survival and their partners know it. Unfortunately, this creates an imbalance of power that interferes with negotiating potential. Think in business terms. Whenever two or more parties come to the negotiation table, if they want the negotiation to be successful—that is, to bring satisfaction to both parties—they should possess equality of power or assets. Without equality, one party will invariably be crushed.

Many women describe feeling squashed by their male partners during negotiations. As Terrie told me, "He knows the kids and I need him and couldn't make it without him. When things get hot, he's quick to remind me where the door is." Unfortunately, there are many men who misuse their financial power and inflict the pain of tyranny on their dependent partner or spouse. While the powerful partner may feel quite cozy in his superior role, it's time to remove the blinders and realize that no relationship can thrive in the face of financial muscle flexing. As I always say, whatever you say and do boomerangs back on you. And while it may feel good to get your power rocks off at your partner's expense, "on the rocks" is where your relationship is going to end up if you don't wake up and take stock.

Oftentimes, a woman can actually help her guy wake up from his "power nap." If you feel as though you have to put up with whatever your mate is dishing out because you can't survive without him, know that you do have the ability to shift the scales of power. Betty Carter and Joan K. Peter's book, *Love, Honor & Negotiate,* describes the impact of inequality in marriage and details how to reclaim your power. When a woman acquires a sense of independence and conveys that she is capable, and willing to take care of herself, this is often all that's needed to help a man wake up to his misuse of power.

Female Power Play: Manipulation

When men misuse their power, it's common for women to resort to the only power play they know: manipulation. Winning is still the unconscious goal, but it's expressed in a subtle way, rather than an overtly aggressive one. Various manipulation cards can be played alone or in conjunction: spending money to get even, refusing sex, threatening abandonment, flirting with other men, withdrawing of love, or guilt trips. Everyone is familiar with these tactics. While they may "work" in the short run because a woman may receive what she wants, manipulation always backfires in the long run. This is because the person on the receiving end of the manipulation feels angry, and anger causes ANS arousal, defensiveness, and withdrawal. In short, no healthy negotiations can occur when a mate is defensive or simply gone.

Why would a woman resort to such ineffective tactics? Sometimes manipulation is all a woman knows.

Lucille's mother was a passive woman who tolerated a drunken, abusive husband. She could never directly address her husband regarding his behavior because of his miserable temper and because she needed his paycheck; instead, she resorted to various manipulations in an attempt to control his behavior. She hid his car keys or faked an illness so that he would be forced to stay home and care for her rather than go out drinking. Lucille learned from her mother that women manipulate in order to get what they want.

Cut to 20 years later. When Lucille feels neglected by her husband, instead of saying directly that she wants attention, she complains that she has a sore shoulder from ironing his shirts, and hopes that he will feel guilty, drop his ball game, and pay attention to her. Unfortunately, her behavior only irritates him and sends him farther away.

Why else do women resort to manipulation rather than negotiation? Many women lack financial power, but what about sexual power? I'm sure you know women whose sexuality is a cannon aimed directly at their spouses. If the husband is "good," he gets it; if he isn't, it's a sexual diet of bread and water and self-service restaurants. When a woman uses sex as a power tool or weapon, it always backfires, and she soon becomes a victim of chronic relationship conflict. The point is, a woman must find a nonsexual way of equalizing the power in her relationship, and until she does, no negotiations are possible.

Amelia felt crushed by her husband. He often stayed out with the boys and was deaf to her pleas and her rage when he returned home. It wasn't until she decided to increase her own power by starting a career that the marriage began to change. Merely beginning school was enough to upset the power apple-cart. Amelia didn't need to threaten divorce or engage in other relationship-destructive acts (like having an affair). She simply moved ahead with her life. This was all that was needed to communicate her message: I refuse to allow you to crush me. I will get on with my life with or without you. This wake-up call was quite effective, because her husband realized that he loved her and didn't want to lose her. He began to improve his behavior and negotiate a more acceptable arrangement.

Often, making the decision that you are ready, willing, and able to move on is sufficient to ring your husband's wake-up bell. Making this simple mental shift causes the seesaw to switch positions; suddenly your husband realizes how much he loves you and drops his muscle flexing.

Equalizing the power is one way to improve your bargaining influence, but there still may be other obstacles to negotiation. These obstacles operate at the level of the couple.

Couple Types and Conflict-Resolution Blocks

In her classic study, M. A. Fitzpatrick identified four basic couple types—*Traditionals, Separates, Independents,* and *Mixed*—and as you will see, each type is prone to its own unique brand of unhealthy conflict negotiations. Understanding your couple type will offer clues to your negotiation roadblocks. The structured negotiation techniques presented later in the book will enable you to steer clear of these blocks.

— **Traditional** couples are like *Ozzie and Harriet*. They have an old-fashioned approach to sex roles and division of household tasks, and they tend to agree on marital and family concerns. Hence, Traditionals have the least amount of relationship conflict. However, conflict still exists. The Traditional wife's tendency to overlook areas of conflict and swallow her feelings places her in danger of becoming depressed or developing psychosomatic illnesses that may include tension headaches, as well as stomach and bowel disturbances. Suppressed feelings may also result in periodic explosions of anger. For such wives, learning to become more direct regarding areas of conflict may become necessary, especially if they are showing signs of fraying around the emotional edges.

— **Separates** are as the name sounds. They tend to be cut off from their mates, spend much time apart, and disclose more of their true feelings to friends. According to research, Separates avoid direct conflict with their mates. It would appear that Separate couples maintain their distance so as not to spark the intense emotions that lurk beneath their veneer of indifference. If both partners are satisfied with this arrangement, no problem exists, at least in the short run. But more often than not, one or both parties wake up—for example, when they meet someone to whom they are attracted—and realize that they have no bond with their partner. In such cases, the relationship quickly dissolves. If Separates decide to brave the sea of emotional distance and address their areas of conflict, they must be sure to first master all partial identification and listening techniques, discussed in Chapters 7 and 8, before attempting any conflict resolution.

— **Independent** couples are assertive in their communications and often find themselves caught in conflicts over big and small issues. There is little agreement on division of household tasks or on the manner and frequency of displays of affection, and they often argue about whether or not to separate and divorce. On surveys, Independents see themselves as self-disclosing, but see their partners as being unwilling to reveal themselves. These couples need to be aware of their tendency to negotiate on trivial matters and learn to distinguish big from small. In addition, since Independents engage in open displays of conflict, they must learn to cool down their communications and, alternatively, listen and self-disclose—activities that are all sorely lacking in the Independents' marriages.

— **Mixed** couples can exhibit any or all of the above characteristics, and they should adopt the recommendations that apply to the couple type they most resemble.

Individual Obstacles

Conflict-resolution blocks can also operate on an individual level. If you want to resolve your conflicts, you must identify and surrender the faulty conflict-resolution tactics that you learned in your family of origin. The following is a list of the faulty tactics that many individuals employ.

Yielding

The person who yields—usually female—attempts to resolve conflicts by committing psychological suicide. She sweeps herself under the rug by surrendering even on issues that are greatly important to her. Reasons for yielding include fear of confrontation, which often stems from feelings of dependency and powerlessness; fear of making her spouse angry; fear of abandonment; low self-esteem (wanting to be liked); or fear of saying or doing horrible things in anger. The yielder often rationalizes her feelings away by telling herself, *It's not important* or *Peace is better than fighting* or *God loves humble people* or *Who am I to impose my views?* or *I love him and must make concessions.*

The following exchange is typical of such couples.

> *Husband:* You are such a lousy cook. How many times do I have to tell you that kitty chow tastes better than your tuna casserole?
> *Wife:* I'm sorry, dear. I'll throw the recipe away.

It's also common for the yielder to put up with all sorts of abuses, never addressing her own feelings of anger. She lives under the illusion that if she silently tolerates whatever garbage is heaped on her, her mate will eventually reward her patience. Instead of being rewarded, the doormat digs a deeper grave for herself, and rather than earning appreciation and love, her tolerance trains her mate to continue abusing her. Meanwhile, the conflict goes unresolved.

Habitual Conflict Avoidance: The Ostrich Policy

This tactic is based on self-deception: fooling oneself into believing that if the problem is ignored, it will go away. For example, a husband comes home late, after having spent hours playing pool at a strip bar with his friends, and the wife, thinking that he'll grow out of the phase, never says a word.

No matter what defenses are used—denial, avoidance, compromise, or soothing—the conflict will continue until it is addressed directly and resolved. Problems never disappear as a result of ignoring them or wishing them away. Moreover, what doesn't get better gets worse, because silent acceptance reinforces the mistreating mate's behavior.

Individuals who habitually avoid conflict do so not by mutual agreement, but because one or both of the partners are afraid of open discord for any of the reasons mentioned in the previous pages. Conflict resolution cannot occur as long as problematic issues are avoided.

Contending

When an individual contends, he or she argues and debates over any issue. The central feature of contending is that every last detail must be disputed. Contending looks like this:

> *"I'm upset about what happened at your mother's last Friday—"*
> *"It was last Thursday."*
> *"Okay, last Thursday. Anyway, when she said that we should save more money—"*
> *"That's not exactly what she said."*

Contenders tear away at each other, detail by detail. No resolution can occur until contending stops.

Lack of Cooperation

Lack of cooperation can be a sign of ANS arousal, or it can also be a clue that Old Scars are intruding. The person who finds it difficult to cooperate may have a weak sense of self and believe that cooperating means loss of identity. At the age of two, most children define their identities by opposing their parents. Saying "no" means *I am me, not you.* If something went awry during this stage of emotional development—if, for example, a child was never allowed to flex his individuation muscles—that person will remain stuck in this stage, and will forever try to make up for what went wrong by refusing to cooperate as an adult.

Your spouse may not cooperate with you for another reason. If your mate's parents never cooperated with each other, he or she will be clueless about how to engage in behavior that was never demonstrated. If chronic uncooperativeness continues after you have applied the healing techniques for this type of Old Scar (see Chapter 5), and even after you have succeeded in cooling down the discussions (see Chapter 7), then professional help is in order.

Controlling

Controlling behavior creates the illusion of conflict resolution, but as I said in my description of the Power Plays Fight Trap, this tactic angers the spouse who is being suppressed, and creates more conflict in the long run. An inability to release the reins conceals a fear of being taken over. In order to help your mate feel safe enough to collaborate with you, you must ask for input at all phases of your conflict discussions. For example, ask "What do you think?" or "What do you suggest?"

Competition: Needing to Win at All Costs

Many distressed spouses approach conflict negotiations like adversaries, both trying to impose their separate agendas. This is what game theorists call the zero-sum game, in which one partner wins all and the other loses all. Couples who employ this tactic will use any or all of the Fight Traps in order to force their opponent to throw in the towel.

Why is winning so important to unhappy couples? In distressed marriages, more energy is placed on winning than on nourishing the relationship and each other. In this emotionally barren environment, both partners' egos erode; one apparent way to bolster a flailing ego is to win. Unfortunately, winning at all costs produces a vicious cycle: the winner's self-esteem is raised, but residual anger in the loser escalates conflict, which further lowers both partners' self-esteem.

In order to move beyond this impasse, one of you must surrender. By ripping the rug out from under your power struggle, it will quickly end—a power struggle takes two to tango. When the power struggle dissolves, negotiations can proceed.

Only Wimps Give In

The belief that only wimps give in to their wives is a common male attitude. We know that men have been socialized to dominate, so it would seem that cultural conditioning underlies a man's difficulty in yielding to his wife.

But there is more than cultural conditioning going on here. Behind a man's wimp phobia is another, deeper fear: the fear of being annihilated. When a man fears giving in, he believes that if he yields to his wife, even once, she will take him over forever and his testicles will hang like trophies on her nightstand. For a man with this fear, his unyielding position helps him live under the illusion that he is in control. If your husband has a wimp phobia, you need to get the point across to him that compromise is not synonymous with castration. He needs to be reassured that you want his needs to be met, and it is not your intent to devour him.

No Team Players

Distressed couples are often unsuccessful in their negotiations because they don't fight for the team. By contrast, happy couples approach the negotiation table as team members, not adversaries. Both individuals must know that a solution that is not acceptable to both is no solution at all. They not only work as a team; they actually treat the relationship like a separate person to be cherished and respected. In all negotiations, both partners are working for a solution that is good for the relationship. If the relationship thrives, then the spouses know that they both will be happy. In unhappy relationships, however, each partner continues to live as a single person. In these cases, the individual's needs, habits, and outside friends are priority one, and the relationship receives the leftovers.

Lack of Creativity

When couples have been fighting for a while, their fights become highly patterned. I explained the scientific basis for this in Chapter 1: chronic conflict leads to a permanent state of ANS arousal, which, in turn, leads to loss of higher-order cognitive functions, including creative thinking. So, we have another vicious cycle going here. So long as your fights remain unresolved, ANS arousal will prevail, which means that you can't count on your husband to come up with a creative solution to your problem.

So what can you do? First, you need to calm down; then you should be able to think creatively. Next, write down every possible solution to your problem that you can think of. If necessary, ask for ideas from friends. Calming down and thinking creatively will put you on the path to resolution.

♡

I have now shown you every Fight Trap and faulty conflict-resolution tactic uncovered in my research. These traps and tactics all have one thing in common: they are the result of acted-out anger. When anger is acted out, it invites a retaliatory action in return. Before long, couples are trapped in a web of revenge and counter-revenge.

The important thing to keep in mind is that no matter what Fight Traps or faulty resolution tactics you favor, sooner or later, they all turn up the heat of your conflicts. The more heated the fights, the more your partner will withdraw, and the more withdrawal there is, the greater the conflict.

I know it is not going to be easy to give up your Fight Traps and faulty resolution tactics. But since you are invested in saving your relationship, you have no choice but to give them up. Here's how you can do this: First, make sure that you have identified your faulty resolution tactics and Fight Traps. Next, make the decision to eliminate them. And from now on, whenever you're angry, pause before you react. This will give you the chance to stop yourself from falling into old, bad habits.

Once you have eliminated your Fight Traps and faulty conflict-resolution tactics, you will probably feel ready to roll up your sleeves and start negotiating. Not so fast. Fasten your seat belt for a major relationship hotbed: The Sex Wars.

Chapter Four

BATTLE OF THE BULGE:

The Sex Wars

I have said so far that most relationship warfare occurs when women complain and nag, and men withdraw. There is one arena, however, in which the tables are often turned: sex. In the first part of this chapter, I explain why heated conflicts throw cold water on a woman's sex drive. Next, I discuss how a lack of understanding of the differences between male and female sexuality leads to specific types of conflicts. And finally, I examine Sex War Games, the heated sexual arguments that usually mask other nonsexual issues.

Anger and Insecurity:
The Best Forms of Birth Control

Many women would shed no tears if they never had sex with their partners again; meanwhile, their husbands chase them, begging and pleading for sex. The battle of the bulge affects millions of marriages and is the main area in which men, as opposed to women, do the demanding. I'm not saying that women never pursue men for sex, and we'll talk later in this chapter about what causes men to lose sexual desire for their wives. But for now, let's discuss the most common scenario: a husband who's hot to trot and a wife with a terminal headache.

The technical term for a low sex drive is *inhibited sexual desire,* and this condition affects countless women. What is it about marriage that leaves many women bereft of sexual appetite?

Lack of security.

The need for security is deeply embedded in a woman's biological programming, and this explains why women have historically chosen men who can provide financially for them and their offspring. In this era of female financial independence, many women no longer need men to financially support them. However, statistical data show us that the instinct to be protected still governs a woman's choice of mate. That is, financially independent women still choose men who are even wealthier than they are. If money talks, then biology screams.

The need for security is not just satisfied by choosing a financially successful mate; a woman also needs to feel secure within her relationship or marriage. When a woman feels worried that the union won't survive (as occurs in a climate of chronic conflict), her body automatically turns off from sex. The last thing she wants is a baby without a father to support it. And while she can have sex and avoid pregnancy, thanks to birth control, her biological programming doesn't realize this. This explains why women who are in the throes of relationship distress experience a sexual shutoff long before they can think about inserting their diaphragms.

Men as Emotional Providers

In order to feel secure in her relationship, a woman needs more than a climate that isn't riddled with arguments. She also needs the guarantee that her partner will stay with her forever. This guarantee was, until recently, satisfied through the traditional institution of marriage, which precluded divorce. But today, divorce has become so common that it creates a basic insecurity in women. As a consequence, in order to feel safe, women now require additional assurance that their relationship will last, "till death do us part."

Since that assurance is no longer derived from the external control of society (marriage is no longer indissoluble), it has to be granted by the man. And the only way that a man can persuade his partner of his total commitment is through frequent reminders of his devotion. What was taken for granted in the past must be explicitly restated, again and again. In other words, the form and scope of providing that is expected from men has drastically expanded. This new expectation is a mutation of women's built-in biological need to be protected and provided for.

Reassuring his partner of his eternal devotion and love is only the first way that a man provides emotional security.

The next step consists of giving his partner evidence that his words of love are not empty sounds intended to make her sexually aroused. These melodies and their intended effects will have a short life if a man does not consistently demonstrate to his partner how important she is to him. When he listens to her feelings—positive or negative—and shows that he cares for her needs, a woman feels that he loves her and wants to stay with her forever.

Even more emotional providing is required. If a man wants to create a total sense of security in his partner, he must also learn to communicate his own negative feelings to her. When a man is silent, a woman worries that he is accumulating a mountain of resentments, and that he may up and leave her one day. By being apprised regularly of his emotional state, she can help him purge these feelings through her understanding, and, if needed, she can change the aspects of her behavior that cause his negative feelings. His consistent feedback provides her with a sense of control over the emotional climate of the relationship, which, in turn, provides a deep sense of security.

When a woman's intimacy needs are not being answered by her partner—when she does not feel responded to, when there is no mutual communication, when there is a climate of indifference, and of course, when there is too much conflict and resentment—her biological warning light goes on and her sex drive clicks off. Her biology tells her: *This man does not feel safe any longer. I don't know whether this relationship will last. If we will be separating, the last thing I want is a child.* This point can't be stressed enough: a woman's sex drive fizzles when she feels emotionally insecure or angry with her mate.

Unfortunately, the emotional connection that a woman needs in order to feel turned on just happens to require a form of relating that men—through no fault of their own—are not trained to provide. So, you begin to see why millions of married women lack sexual desire and why conflicts arise in this arena. Don't get me wrong. I'm not saying that women shouldn't wish for greater emotional connection. All I'm saying is that society hasn't trained men to fulfill this new cultural expectation. But don't worry—your partner will be an expert Emotional Provider before I'm finished with him.

If men want their partners to be sexually open to their ardent approaches, and grant willingly the sexual embrace they crave, they will follow my advice. Otherwise, they will be sexually frustrated and locked in futile fights over sex.

Sexual arguments may also arise from a misunderstanding of the nature of male sexuality, the subject I next discuss.

Security vs. Variety

One of the biggest insecurity triggers, and a potent source of marital conflict, arises when a woman does not understand male sexual biology. I remember overhearing a conversation between two men that went like this:

> *Mike:* Have you ever been so sick that you turned your wife down?
> *Fred:* Once I was so sick I turned her down.
> *Mike:* I could have a 105 fever and I wouldn't turn my wife down.
> *Fred:* I said *sick!*

This conversation expresses the essence of male sexual biology. In each ejaculation, 300 million critters are sent swimming upstream to meet only one egg. Once that egg is fertilized, a woman is out of commission for nearly a year. But for the rest of his life, a man can impregnate a new woman each and every day (and twice on Sunday). Men have endless supplies of sperm, and the sperm is often manufactured until death. Women have a limited number of eggs, can only become impregnated a few days each month, and can only reproduce for a portion of their lives.

In order to ensure the continuance of the species, male sexual biology was designed so that they could impregnate as many females as possible. A man's sexual biology is like the supermarket grocery scanner. The goal: process as much merchandise as quickly as possible. But what does all this mean in modern relationship terms? Simply stated, men are not wired for monogamy. It's their love for their partners that keeps them faithful despite tremendous biological programming. The way men express their love is by seeking sexual variety within the relationship. They often want sex in different locations and in kinky ways or positions. Some even like their partners to dress up like other women. Women often react to these requests with hurt feelings. *Why aren't I enough for you? You don't truly love me.*

Actually, by attempting to accommodate his biological urges with his partner, rather than seeking satisfaction elsewhere, a man is saying, "I love you."

I know that all this biology talk sounds like I'm reducing humans to apes—or sperm and eggs. By exaggerating a little, I'm trying to help you understand how the basic differences between men and women's sexuality fuels sexual conflict. Understanding the biological underpinnings of your sexual battles is the first step toward resolution.

Different Sexual Tastes

Now let's move beyond biology to see if we can understand what else may be causing your sexual battles. Very often, couples clash over differing sexual tastes: one likes oral sex, while it's not the other's cup of tea; a husband likes anal sex, but his wife starts packing whenever the subject comes up. Neither partner is right or wrong, but differing values and tastes are often a source of great conflict. When couples get locked in struggles surrounding their particular bone (or should I say boner?) of contention, these fights can get very nasty.

> *Only one year after Carole and John tied the knot, Carole's stomach was in knots. John had been working late for months (hoping to land a management position in his accounting firm), and even during his time off, his nose was buried in records. What's more, he had developed a strange sexual disorder, which Carole called "premature intercourse." He rushed into sex before she was ready, finished the "job" quickly, and then sank into a steady snore, drooling into his pillow. At first, Carole felt hurt and drenched her own pillow with tears. But soon her hurt transformed to anger.*
>
> *One night, after John had his orgasm, she tapped him on the shoulder, and snarled through her curled upper lip, "Say, Mr. Accountant . . . ever heard about the substantial penalties for early withdrawal?"*
>
> *"Very funny. Since you're such an expert, you must know why they call getting married 'tying the knot.'"*
>
> *"Edify me!"*
>
> *"That's what happens to a man's dick!"*

Carole and John's sexual conflicts have become what I call Sex War Games. But don't be fooled—when sex has become your battleground, it's no game.

Sex War Games

Have you ever wondered why many couples resort to playing out their resentments in the sexual arena? Research shows that of all human relationships, marriage produces the most intense emotional reactions, especially anger. When anger enters the scene, you've got problems because, if you're like most people, you don't know how to communicate your anger constructively. As I said before, most people *act* on their anger, which invites action in return—usually revenge or retaliation. Revenge and retaliation are behavioral paybacks ("I'll get even with you because you did this to me"). The goal is to hit each other below the belt. And—you guessed it—slamming each other sexually is the ultimate below-the-belt blow.

Female Sex War Games

Elaine is hot—not sexually, but under the collar. For five years she has been trying to get Patrick to understand that she needs more preparation before intercourse. By this point, she is so fed up and tired of arguing with this man who doesn't get it that she has decided to get even: she will refuse him sex and teach him a little lesson along the way.

On Sunday morning, Patrick offered to do the dishes, a sure sign that his arousal had reached atomic proportions. Now was her chance.

*As he dried the last dish, Patrick smiled and said,
"Honey, how about a little nookie?"*

*"How about a little appetizer before the entrée!"
she snarled as she sorted the laundered socks.*

*"What's that supposed to mean?" he said, grow-
ing beet red.*

"I mean, no sex until I get some decent foreplay."

"I give you foreplay."

*"Give me a break. You're one of the original min-
ute men!"*

*"Why can't you admit that you're freakin' frigid.
My other girlfriends never complained!" he shouted.*

"They were too busy faking it to complain!"

Placing Patrick on a bread-and-water sexual diet is
Elaine's way of punishing him. For centuries, the only
power a woman had was her sexuality. In the play *Lysistrata*
by Aristophanes, the Athenian women refused sex to end a
war. Throughout the ages, women have been able to force
men to slay dragons, rob banks, marry them—or whatever else they wanted. Despite the fact that modern women
have more power than in previous eras, many women still
handle their sexuality like a power tool. You can't believe
how many times a week I hear unhappily married wives
tell me, "I'll fix him. I won't give him any." Another variant
of this approach is "I won't give him oral sex" or "I won't
fix myself up for him." Wives who use this form of revenge
don't realize that they are actually punishing themselves,
because revenge begets revenge.

Male Sex War Games

Men rarely withhold sex as a way of obtaining revenge against their wives. (Even if they wanted to say no to sex, they have to contend with 300 million sperm urging them to take the plunge!) So, how do most men get even with their partners?

We know that women become hurt and angry when their intimacy needs are not met. Men become angry and prone to revenge when their needs for recognition and appreciation aren't being met. You can see the scenario. The woman, feeling that her partner isn't meeting her emotional or sexual needs, starts to complain about his behavior. There goes the man's needed recognition and admiration. I'm not speaking now about whether or not he deserves recognition. All I am saying is that when men feel "bitched at" by their wives, two things happen: (1) they lose motivation to give their partners what they want (foreplay, more cuddling, better communication); and (2) they seek appreciation outside the relationship, usually in the form of an affair. If you ask a man why he had an affair, 99 percent of the time it was not because he wasn't getting enough sex; it was because he wasn't receiving enough appreciation from his partner.

Sex as the Battleground for Nonsexual Issues: How to Read Between the Sheets

When one or both partners are engaged in Sex Wars, I always suspect that something else is on the fritz in the marriage. No matter what the overt sexual struggle is, Sex War Games are often symbolic expressions of other underlying issues, such as a fear of intimacy, dependency, abandonment, or loss of control.

Jack loved his wife, Yvonne, but there was only one problem. He wanted nearly constant sex, and his wife wasn't willing to accommodate him. Soon, he stopped asking her for sex and began having multiple affairs. Yvonne was in a state of despair. She thought Jack wasn't attracted to her anymore, and she couldn't understand why he stopped approaching her for sex. She tried to do the approaching, attempted to introduce sexual variety, and had a total makeover, all to no avail. The couple came to me on the verge of divorce.

It was clear that Jack's need for constant and varied sex had a deeper meaning. It was time for some bedroom detective work, so I used my Reading Between the Sheets technique to figure out what Jack's sexual insatiability really meant. I asked him:

- How did he feel when he didn't have as much sex as he liked?
- How did he feel when he fulfilled his desires with strange women? Did this satisfy him?
- What was he missing in the marriage, if anything?
- What was he missing within himself?
- What hole was he trying to fill (no pun intended) by having sex with numerous women?

By delving into Jack's background, I discovered that his father was a womanizer and that he had abandoned his son and the family when Jack was very young. By following in his father's philandering footsteps, Jack unconsciously lived with his father at his side. So his acts of infidelity were driven by the unconscious wish to fill his inner void. The problem was that by cheating on his wife, he was jeopardizing the love that was waiting for him at home. When Jack understood this, a miracle occurred. He was able to give up his extracurricular affairs and lived, literally, happily ever after from that day forward.

The point to keep in mind here is that sexual conflicts are rarely about what they seem. Take as another example the issue I promised to discuss earlier in this chapter—the battle of the bulge in reverse.

Steve was a man who had lost all his sexual desire for his wife. On the surface, it was easy to assume theirs was a sexual problem. Maybe his wife, Joanne, had let herself go; maybe sex had become routine; or maybe he had too much stress at work. I resisted the temptation to assume that this was the case. Once again, I used my Reading Between the Sheets technique to delve beneath the surface by asking:

- How long had the problem been going on?
- What had changed in the couple's life and relationship?
- Was sex ever good between them? If so, when did it deteriorate?

I learned that their sex life had been fine until the birth of their first child. But Steve's deflated drive wasn't caused by the usual culprits (unresolved anger, stress, illness, exhaustion, or the fact that his wife had become less attractive). So we needed to explore further how the birth of his child was related to his "limp loins" syndrome. Steve recalled a childhood memory in which his mother was standing in front of him in a daffodil-colored dress. He remembered feeling a rush of sexual sensations and then felt struck by a bolt of guilt. Now, we had the key to the puzzle. When Joanne became "Mother," his unconscious guilt over being attracted to his own mother caused him to turn off sexually to his wife. When Steve was able to recognize the deeper issue that was operating, when he realized that it was no sin to have felt attracted to his own mother, he was then able to allow himself to once again feel attraction for his wife.

When it comes to applying my Reading Between the Sheets technique to your own conflicts, it's impossible for me to give you a list of rote questions. Your questions will always change according to the issues you're addressing. But once you understand that your goal is to delve beneath the surface, to get at the emotional core that underlies your sexual struggle, the right questions will come naturally to you.

Reading Between the Sheets is like peeling the layers of an onion. On the first layer, we discover that sexual battles often reflect deeper relationship issues that have nothing to do with sex. Then, when we peel off the next layer, we discover that heated sexual conflicts are fueled by other, deeper scars from childhood. In the next chapter, I will systematically address these Old Scars.

♥ ♥ ♥

Chapter Five

BATTLE SCARS:

How Childhood Wounds Cause Chronic Relationship Conflict and How to Heal Them

Chronic relationship fighting is caused by the Old Scars of childhood. In this chapter, I will help you identify the specific early wounds that are creating your relationship distress and show you effective ways to heal them.

I speak of effective healing because the unconscious mind, left to its own devices, has an ineffective way of attempting to heal our psychological traumas: to replay, with our partner, the painful events of the past in the hope of achieving a better outcome this time around. Unfortunately, our efforts usually fail, and bitter arguments are the sad result. But our need to heal drives us to try again and again, to no avail. This leads to fight repetition, when the same fights occur regularly, and intense arguing—the two clues that Old Scars lurk beneath the surface and are adding fuel to your fights.

Repetition: The First Clue

The first way we re-create our early traumas is by choosing a mate who emotionally resembles the parent who was the source of our pain. Realize that even the most beloved parent will unintentionally fail and even traumatize his or her child. I know you may be thinking, *I didn't choose my husband because he's like my father or mother. I picked him because he has great buns or makes a great macaroni salad.* These are the conscious aspects of mate selection. But in actuality, mate selection is primarily driven by the unconscious motivation to choose someone who possesses traits that resemble the parent who injured us. I call this Setting the Stage. We Set the Stage not because we are gluttons for punishment, but because the unconscious has a master plan: to replay our childhood traumas with a person who symbolizes the parent who injured us, and to work for what I call a Happy Ending to that trauma.

> Janel's father abused her verbally. Not surprisingly, she married a man who belittled her daily. She came to see me, depressed, not understanding why she was treated so horribly by her husband.
>
> By marrying a verbally abusive man, Janel unconsciously hoped to transform him into a person who treated her with respect and love. If she could pull this off, it would feel as if she succeeded in making her

*father come around—and her original trauma would
be healed.*

That plan looks good on paper, but rarely works in real
life, for two reasons. First, when we choose partners who
resemble our parents, we soon discover that our mates are
incapable of providing the emotional responses we need,
precisely because they are damaged or limited in the exact
same areas that our parents were.

The second reason our healing attempts fail is that we
adopt with our partners the same strategies that we employed with our parents. And given that our methods didn't
succeed with our parents, they sure aren't going to hit the
jackpot with our mates. We soon feel frustrated, hurt, and
furious. But since our unconscious goal is to heal at any
cost, we stay in the ring and keep swinging. The need to
engage in repeated healing attempts is so universal that it
actually has a name: the Repetition Compulsion.

Intensity: The Second Clue

Fight intensity is another clue that unfinished business
lurks beneath the surface of your fights. It goes without
saying that each time you battle through the same fight
and lose, you are more aggravated than the time before.
But there is another reason for the intensity of your reactions. In a nutshell, the unconscious mind constantly links
present-day slights with the wounds you suffered as a kid.
This is what I call the Emotional Lake Effect. Think about an
actual lake-effect blizzard that gathers moisture and energy
as it moves across large expanses of warmer lake water and
dumps mounds of snow on the lake's leeward shores. Well,
the unconscious mind does the same thing. As the mind

dips into the reservoir of your unconscious, it dredges up memories of similar hurts that you suffered as a kid. The next thing you know, you're blowing an emotional gasket because you are reliving *all* the pain of previous similar offenses. This explains why fireworks are going off inside you even though the current event doesn't seem to warrant such an explosive reaction.

To complicate matters, these associations are happening on an unconscious level, meaning your "feeling memories" are disembodied from the actual events. As a result, it's easy to mistakenly assume that the mountain of emotions you're experiencing is the result of whatever your partner just said or did. The next thing you know, you're aiming your broadsides at your partner and dumping old emotional baggage onto him or her without realizing it. This heats the environment to a sizzle.

> *Bob repeatedly checks his office messages when he is out with Mary. Mary becomes increasingly agitated by this behavior and finally blows up at him.*

Why is she so furious over a seemingly innocuous action? Because this experience with Bob triggers memories of her mother, who never had time for her. So when a trivial incident occurs in the present, it surges that already overloaded circuit in her brain, and she blows. Such associations usually occur without any conscious awareness.

Old Scars Test

Before we go further, let's determine whether your arguments are being fueled by Old Scars. Take the following test.

The subjects that we fight about are repetitive in nature.	T or F
I find myself and/or my partner becoming intensely upset over little things, and I can't understand why.	T or F
I find myself and/or my partner using the same words, explanations, and fighting tactics during our spats, even though these methods never work.	T or F
I always end up with the same feelings before, during, and after our fights.	T or F
Our fights seem familiar to me, but I can't put my finger on why.	T or F
I feel that there is a scripted nature to our fights and that I can actually predict their same sorry outcome.	T or F
I remember fighting with my parent(s) and feeling the same emotions that I feel now when I fight with my mate.	T or F
The feelings that I have after a fight with my partner remind me of how I felt as a kid.	T or F

If you answered *true* to more than one of the questions above, Old Scars are contributing your fights. But you still may feel at a loss to understand what piece of your history is being played out through your marital conflicts. It is often difficult to determine the issues that underlie your arguments because the fight content operates like a smoke screen. When you're arguing over dirty socks or pots and pans, it's very difficult to abstract from these concrete subjects and see what's "underneath" your fights.

To assist you in this process, I have developed a technique that I call Drawing a Fight Map, which enables you to strip away the overt fight content. Just as a restorer strips the outer layers of paint from an object to reveal the original finish, you can go beneath the outer layer (the overt content) of your fight to reveal the underlying traumas that lurk below.

Stripping Away the Fight Content

In order to determine what traumas lie beneath your overt fight (who did what to whom), you need to flesh out, on paper, the emotional mapping of the conflict. To do this, you must forget the apparent content of the fight—the cold Chinese food, the rushed foreplay—and instead study the emotional content.

Let me show you one of Nancy and Phil's overt fights. Then I will draw upon their example to explain how you can strip away the content of your fights.

The Overt Fight

"Why can't you take me out sometimes? Would it kill you to make me happy?" Nancy whined.
"No, it wouldn't kill me!" Phil snapped.
"So, what's your problem?"

"God, I'm so busy with work, and you're worried about stupid outings!"

"It's not stupid. It's important to me, and that should matter to you!"

"You matter. Why do you think I work as hard as I do?"

"What's work got to do with my feelings? You don't care about me at all."

"That's right. I don't care about you at all. I don't stay out drinking, I don't cheat, but I don't care!" John shouted as he stormed from the room.

"God, I can't talk to you. You just won't listen!"

Drawing a Fight Map

Step 1: Chart the Emotional Course of the Fight

In the first step, think of one of your common fights. For the moment, forget the content of the fight and focus on the feelings it stirs in you. Write down these feelings.

Let's see how Nancy and Phil stripped away the overt fight content to reveal the emotional mapping of their issue.

From Nancy's perspective: I want something from Phil. He makes excuses as to why he can't give me what I want. I get angry. He becomes more defensive. I get angrier. He digs in his heels even further. I feel hurt that he doesn't love me enough to listen and change the behaviors that annoy me. So I press harder and harder, and he withdraws further and further into excuses and denial.

From Phil's perspective: When Nancy wants something from me, she orders me around and manipulates me. She gives me no freedom whatsoever. I have to do exactly as she wants or else she's furious. I feel angry, like a trapped animal. I feel like running to escape her rage and demands.

Step 2: Recognize the Feelings That You Experienced in Childhood

Next, ask yourself, *Does the fight with my mate stir the same feelings I felt as a child?* Write these feelings down. Then, ask yourself, *Who triggered these feelings in me?*

Let's see what Nancy and Phil came up with for this step.

Nancy recalled feeling impotent, frustrated, hurt, and angry when she tried—unsuccessfully—to get her father to respond to her.

Phil felt controlled by his mother and enraged by how she forced him to do her will. Whenever he defied her, he had to suffer her fury and threats of abandonment.

Step 3: Recall a Specific Childhood Memory

Next, uncover an early memory in which you felt the way you feel when you argue with your mate. With whom were you struggling? What happened? How did the fight play out? Write this down.

Here's how Nancy and Phil handled this step.

Nancy recalled pleading with her father to come to at least one of her softball games. He never showed. She begged and cried, but he never relented.

Phil remembered his mother forcing him to clean his room on a sunny day. When he resisted, she shouted at him and locked him in his room without supper.

Step 4: Identify the Type of Treatment You Yearned for from Your Parent(s)

This step identifies your Happy Ending. So finally, most important of all, ask yourself, *How did I wish my struggles with my parent(s) had worked out? Did I wish that my parent(s) would apologize or see my point of view? Did I wish my parent(s) would compromise?* Clearly identify your desired outcome. Write this down.

Let's return to Nancy and Phil for this last step.

Nancy wished her father had responded to her requests, at least sometimes.

Phil needed to feel free to assert himself without being punished.

Once you've identified the treatment you desired from your parent(s), you have a fairly clear understanding of what your mind is hoping to accomplish in your fights with your mate (your Happy Ending).

The question now becomes: Why don't most of us succeed in obtaining our Happy Endings? Why, for example, hasn't Nancy succeeded in obtaining what she needs from Phil?

Remember, Phil is just like Nancy's father. And she relates to him the way she related to her dad. For example, she used to scream, yell, pout, and whine at her father, without effect. Since Phil resembles her father, it doesn't take a brain surgeon to figure out why Nancy's methods aren't cutting it. The fact that she has chosen a mate like her father cannot be changed, but what can be changed is her way of dealing with him. In other words, this aspect of the Repetition Compulsion (adopting the same strategies that she used with her father) is under Nancy's control. And if she wishes to achieve her Happy Ending, she will modify her way of relating to Phil. The two principles that follow will help Nancy—and you—chart a new course of action.

Achieve Your Happy Ending

1. Know Your Mate's Old Scars

If you're in the dark when it comes to what makes your mate tick, you risk unwittingly ripping open his Old Scars, in which case he will be nursing his own wounds and will be unavailable to resolve your conflicts. If necessary, redo the last exercise, answering the questions as you believe your mate would. This process will help you identify his early wounds.

When Nancy did this, she recalled that Phil's mother's child-rearing methods fell into the "My way or the highway" approach. Hence, his early wound relates to never having been given sufficient autonomy.

Although Nancy hadn't realized it before, her manner of handling her husband—demanding, pressuring, and so on—was painfully reminiscent of the way Phil's mother dealt with him. Nancy had to face the fact that her pressure tactics were making Phil dig his heels in deeper.

The question became: How could Nancy help Phil be more responsive to her? She could provide him with a communication style that gives him a feeling of choice. One possibility would be for Nancy to ask him for suggestions on how to solve their problem. Doing so would put him in the driver's seat, and if he felt in charge, rather than controlled, he would become more responsive to her. Understanding Phil's early wounds was Nancy's first step on the road to resolving their fights, and healing her own Old Scars as well.

As for Phil, establishing an open dialogue with Nancy, in which they agree that he can point out to her whenever he experiences her as pressuring him the way his mother did, would not only help Nancy to be more considerate of him, but would also assist him in healing his Old Scar with his mom, which would further enable him to be more responsive to her.

2. Discuss Your Old Scars

To attenuate the intensity of your fights, you need to explain to your mate that an Old Scar is adding fuel to your fire. Directing the focus off his ego and onto historical sources minimizes the risk of ANS arousal and frees your mate to support you and resolve your conflicts instead of defending himself. Let's turn to another example—that of Dottie and Russell.

A major turning point for Dottie and Russell occurred when I encouraged her to explain how his behavior was reminiscent of her mother's. Russell was stiff and speechless, and Dottie was beet red.

"Explain to Russell what he's doing that reminds you of your mother," I urged.

"If I tried to tell my mother how I felt, she'd lock me in my room," Dottie said tearfully.

"I didn't know that," Russell answered.

"Tell Russell specifically what he is doing that reminds you of your mother," I once again urged.

"When you tell me, 'Don't be upset, it's no big deal,' my blood boils. . . . It's like my mother telling me to shut up!"

"I had no idea!" Russell paled with emotion. *"I always wanted to make life better for you than it was with your mother."*

When Russell's ego was taken off the hook—when he realized that the intensity of Dottie's pain and anger was the result of childhood traumas—he felt more willing to support her, rather than withdraw. This seemingly simple communication—telling your mate what old hurts have been activated by his behavior—has helped curtail withdrawal reactions for most of the men in my case studies. Try it yourself and see the miracles that occur.

On the following pages, I will outline the most common Old Scars and offer specific healing suggestions. Keep in mind that if Old Scars are being expressed through drug or alcohol abuse, or if physical violence has entered the scene, professional help must be sought.

OLD SCAR #1

"Where are you, Mommy [Daddy]?"
"Please pay attention to me, Mommy [Daddy]."

When you were young, your parents separated or divorced, and you were emotionally or physically abandoned by one or both parents. Mom or Dad never had time for you, vanished without a trace, popped in and out at whim, or promised to visit and never showed up.

How This Old Scar Often Surfaces in Relationship Conflicts: A, B, C, D

(A) Usually female: *excessive clinginess*

If abandonment is a part of your history, you may be clingy or possessive, demanding more of your partner's time than he is willing to give or requesting constant reassurances that you are important to him.

(B) Male or female: *jealousy*

You may feel that your mate loves another person more than you, even though you have no reason to suspect infidelity. You may feel jealous of his involvement with other people or of the time he devotes to the kids, friends, or hobbies.

(C) Male or female: *acting-out behaviors*

You or your mate may engage in behaviors designed to fill the emptiness inside: excessive drinking or spending, overeating, promiscuous sex, or extramarital affairs. If either partner's behavior is out of control, professional help is needed.

(D) Often male (but can occur with females): *fears of intimacy or dependency*

The person who was abandoned as a child may behave in ways that keep his mate at arm's length—working compulsively, avoiding family outings or vacations, or missing family meals. The unconscious goal is to avoid intimacy at all costs in order to protect oneself: *If I am cut off emotionally, then I won't suffer when I'm abandoned again.*

Type of Healing Needed

For A, B

You need to know that your mate will not abandon you the way your parent(s) did. Additionally, you must feel that you are number one in your partner's eyes. Remember, it's hard for your mate to offer this message if he feels blamed for infidelity or neglect. Also, keep in mind that actions or omissions that may slightly annoy someone else will devastate you because of your history. You must tell your spouse that your accusations of infidelity or neglect have been fueled by childhood abandonment. When the blame is directed away from his ego, he won't feel compelled to defend himself and can devote his energy to offering the assurances you need. These principles also apply if the husband is the jealous partner.

For C

If either of you is acting out in order to fill an internal void, strong limits must be set around the unacceptable behavior. At the same time, a great deal of emotional nourishment must be provided.

Chet regularly came home drunk and forced sex on his wife, Eva. For years, she tolerated his behavior.

Then, when he fell asleep, she searched for the abandoned car, which he had been too drunk to drive home. The next day she yelled at him, but also called in sick for him, using some bogus excuse. Without knowing it, she was rewarding Chet's destructive behavior. After talking with me, we devised a plan. No sex for him if he was drunk, and no sweeping up behind him, either. He would have to find the car himself and call his boss. I instructed Eva to give him no attention whatsoever, including negative attention (yelling, screaming), when he acted badly and to stop bailing him out. The result: within a few months, he stopped drinking and cleaned up his act considerably.

The limits that Eva imposed on her husband were firm and consistent, and not presented in the form of screaming and yelling. This is an important point, because even negative attention has the effect of reinforcing behavior.

In addition to ignoring inappropriate behavior, I encouraged Eva to praise Chet's positive behaviors. I know it's hard to praise someone who still continues to behave in unacceptable ways, but keep in mind that no matter how badly your partner may be behaving, there is always something that you can find to praise. You might just be so angry that you aren't noticing the good things.

Even if you don't feel like it, do offer emotional support, recognition, and praise whenever your partner behaves more properly, and especially give praise for the little gains. In Eva's case, she recognized Chet for taking the responsibility to call in sick. When you praise the little gains, this encourages your partner to make bigger gains. In fact, many studies, including my own research, have shown that people change their behavior when they are rewarded, whereas punishment (nagging, yelling, screaming, and the like) has no effect on improving behavior.

For D

If your spouse was abandoned as a child, he still lives in fear of being abandoned again. So he backs off to protect himself, thinking that if he's emotionally detached, he won't suffer when you leave him. You need to help him see that if he isn't careful, he may arrange to make his worst fear come true: his protective mechanism may backfire because his pulling back pushes you away.

In order to heal, he needs to allow himself to connect to you. But before he can do so, he requires an emotional insurance policy that protects him against being abandoned by you. At the same time, he needs to know that whenever he feels too frightened by the closeness, you will allow him to back away, temporarily. Before withdrawing, he needs to explain that he is backing off to deal with his own fears, not to escape you or the family.

You can tell him the following: "I just want to reassure you that I'm not going anywhere. I also want you to know that if you take the risk to get closer to me, I will give you breathing room anytime you need it. So long as I understand why you are pulling away—to handle your own fears, not to escape me—I will happily give you your space."

OLD SCAR #2

"Mommy [Daddy], get off my back."

You grew up with an overly controlling or intrusive parent who told you when to do your homework, what friends you could play with, what sports you could engage in, or what hobbies you should perform.

How This Old Scar Often Surfaces in Relationship Conflicts: A, B, C

(A) Male or female: *tyrannical behavior*
A person who felt controlled as a child will likely become a tyrant in adulthood, copying the behavior of a bossy parent. Overly controlling behavior is a defense against being controlled.

(B) Male or female: *uncooperative behavior*
Various power struggles may crop up, and you or your partner will have difficulty yielding, compromising, or considering the other's point of view. Fights will run on forever, and the tyrannical partner will use pressure and manipulation tactics in order to impose his or her desires or position.

(C) Often female: *excessive compliance*
If you were dominated as a child, you may behave in overtly compliant ways and allow your partner to rule you. Privately, you struggle with feelings of victimization, helplessness, or anger.

Type of Healing Needed

For A, B

The person who was dominated as a child needs to experience the feeling of independence that was lacking in childhood. It is common for the overly controlled child to become a tyrant in adult life: *No one is going to boss me. Everything is going to be my way.* If you are on the receiving end of a tyrant, the natural reaction is to resist the commands. Before long, you become trapped in endless tugs-of-war. The challenge here is to resist digging in your heels and becoming the stubborn parent your mate grew up with. Instead, transform your mate into your consultant and regularly seek his opinion on how he recommends dealing with your conflicts. If you do this, he will feel considered and will be less likely to force his will down your throat.

I know it's not a natural tendency to yield when you're fighting with someone who won't consider your position or contemplate a compromise. To declare a truce to the tug-of-war requires a lot of maturity on your part, but remember, by temporarily backing off, you're providing your partner with the necessary emotional healing. Soon he will feel satisfied that his needs have been respected and will be ready to consider your needs. By backing off, you have, in fact, modeled for your partner how to respect another person's feelings. As long as you maintain the tug-of-war, you are unwittingly playing the role of the controlling parent, and your partner will never have a chance to heal the wound and grow up.

The yielding on your part should not become a permanent solution to the conflicts. It's only temporary and is designed to provide your partner with the feeling that he can have things his way—not through winning a fight, but because you love him enough to give him the respect and consideration he never had as a kid. After a while, your partner should be more willing to give equal time to your needs.

For C

Your healing requires that you become an equal partner. In doing so, you may be jeopardizing your marriage, which has probably been built upon a power imbalance.

Realize that your partner chose you because you allowed him or her to dominate you, and his or her ego thrives on feeling superior, needed, and important. How will your partner react to your gaining more equality? Be prepared for the risks before you assert yourself. If you decide that you're ready, go slowly.

Begin by talking about your need for more of a voice in the marriage. For example, participate in the financial planning or in the establishment of a budget. And be prepared for much balking on your partner's part. He or she may be afraid to relinquish control. The resistance may also conceal a fear that once you become more independent, you won't need him or her any longer. So, as you take your full place in the marriage, you need to keep telling your partner how important he or she is to you and how much you continue to need him or her. If you sense that your mate is frightened by the loss of control, then make sure to keep asking for his or her opinions and suggestions.

OLD SCAR #3

"Mommy [Daddy], why can't I just play?"

You were robbed of your childhood by being forced to assume too much responsibility too young. You might have done all the housework, or perhaps you had to care for siblings or parents who were physically ill, emotionally disturbed, or chemically dependent.

How This Old Scar Often Surfaces in Relationship Conflicts: A, B

(A) Usually male: *irresponsible behavior*
A refusal to accept adult responsibilities: paying bills late, not keeping promises, not following the law or rules.

(B) Often female: *over-responsible behavior*
If you assumed the caretaker role in childhood, you will probably take an over-responsible attitude in your marriage. Since your parents were unable to assume adequate responsibility for you, you would have drowned if you hadn't stayed in charge. As an adult, you continue assuming all of the duties of your household. Beneath the over-responsible attitude is a fear that life will fall apart if you give over the reins. You may also fear that your mate won't be able to handle his share of things. Since you're carrying too much responsibility in the relationship, you feel resentment toward your partner and may even fight with him for his not doing his share of the household tasks.

Type of Healing Needed

For A

Your partner needs to experience the fun and freedom he never enjoyed as a child. The challenge for you is not to fall into the role of the nagging and controlling parent. If you fall into this trap, your mate's need to rebel will constantly be refueled by you. The best plan is to remove yourself from the hot seat by allowing him to fall flat on his face. This is difficult to do because many of your mate's irresponsible actions will boomerang on you. You may want to take some measures to protect yourself—like setting up separate checking accounts.

Once you've put your damage control in place, make sure not to bail out your "kid" when he gets into a tight spot. Let him get himself out. And make sure that you don't fall in the trap of scolding him for his mistakes. Ignore them—otherwise you will be reinforcing his behavior through negative attention. If you can tolerate this process, his irresponsible actions will usually be short-lived. When he has to suffer the consequences of his actions, he'll soon find that having so much fun is too big a pain.

Realize that "letting go" and not bailing your mate out will probably be especially difficult for you because your over-responsibility probably re-creates patterns you learned in childhood (familiar pain).

For B

You need to give over responsibility to your mate gradually until there is a more equal division of tasks. In the beginning, you'll probably still need to tell your partner how you prefer the work done. You must realize, however, that men especially don't like being told how to perform tasks. So make sure that your suggestions don't come across as controlling or bossy. You also need to let your mate know that your "how-to" suggestions, if followed, will help you surrender the reins more easily and make you less angry at him.

There's usually a fly in the ointment with this type of problem. It's not uncommon for the "do-it-all" type of woman to become committed to someone she can't rely on, so giving over the reins to such a person would, in fact, be risky. If you can't count on your mate, you'll need to follow the healing suggestions for Old Scar #4.

OLD SCAR #4

"Mommy [Daddy], you don't care what I do."

Your partner wasn't given enough limits or responsibility (his parents never set a curfew, for instance, or never made him do his homework or chores).

How This Old Scar Often Surfaces in Relationship Conflicts

Many male children are treated like kings by mothers who never stop taking care of them. Men who have been raised in this way suffer from what psychoanalysts call an "oral dependency," meaning that they are fixated in the oral stage of development. And these men come to marriage expecting their wives to take over where their mothers left off—kind of like switching from the right breast to the left breast. With this type of man, you are dealing with a two-pronged problem: a developmental sticking point and a culture-bound socialization that may be part of your mate's personality makeup. He'll usually come and go as he pleases, play hard, and assume no responsibility for household chores or money management. If you're on the receiving end of this behavior, you may fall into the role of the nagging, complaining wife.

Type of Healing Needed

To help your mate become more responsible, you'll gradually need to do less for him and praise him for any responsible actions he takes on his own. Don't expect him to become Mr. Responsible overnight. He was, after all, rewarded as a child for not being responsible; and you rewarded him, too, by allowing his behavior to continue until recently. Your challenge is how to make him feel rewarded for being responsible now.

Humans grow when enough love and encouragement is offered. I know it may sound silly to think of your partner as a child needing positive reinforcement. You may be thinking, *It's not my job to be his mother,* but you're already being his mother by taking on most of the responsibility and nagging him like a parent. You are a negative mother to him. How about trying to be a positive mother? Remember, he'll need a lot of praise from you to give up a way of being that feels pretty damn good.

If you feel like digging in your heels and not giving him what he needs, you should examine how this resistance connects to your own past. Maybe your parents tried to teach you by punishing bad behavior rather than positively reinforcing good behavior. If this is true, you may be tempted to use the same methods with your mate. If you insist upon teaching him through negative messages, punishment, and taking away what he likes, you'll have a child for life. Until you can move beyond your sticking point, he won't be able to grow. Not to mention the fact that if you punish him too much, he could get fed up and leave.

Didn't he marry you because he knew you would fill the responsible role in your marriage? If the answer is yes, and if you decide to change the rules midstream, you have to go about this slowly and in a positive fashion. You can help your partner become more mature and responsible by adopting the following steps.

1. Offer no more positive attention for irresponsible behavior. This includes bailouts, cleanups, and so on.

2. Offer no more negative attention for irresponsible behavior. This includes screaming, yelling, and the like.

3. Give no attention whatsoever to immature behavior. Pretend you're deaf, dumb, and blind. (This is very hard to do when you feel like killing your mate. Just keep saying to yourself, *This is temporary, and it will work!*)

4. Reward your mate's responsible behaviors with words of praise, signs of affection, and positive attention.

5. Remember to reward the baby steps. Very often wives expect overnight results (after all, he is an adult). Keep in mind that we all must

crawl before we walk. And no matter what age your mate is, if he never learned to walk on his own, he must learn to crawl now. Make sure that each tentative step is rewarded with praise.

OLD SCAR #5

"Mommy [Daddy], stop yelling at me."
"Mommy [Daddy], stop hitting me."

How This Old Scar Often Surfaces in Relationship Conflicts: A, B

(A) Male or female: *victimization*
Formerly abused people are in danger of behaving in abusive ways.

(B) Usually female: *victimhood*
If you were abused as a child, you risk becoming a victim in adulthood.

Type of Healing Needed

For A

If you or your partner grew up with abusive parents, you probably never learned how to handle angry feelings in nondestructive ways. See Chapter 9 for a complete discussion of how to communicate negative feelings effectively.

If you were abused as a child, you may find yourself wanting to get even with the parent who mistreated you—and you may find yourself dumping on your partner. The risk of this happening increases when your partner unconsciously reminds you of the parent whom you resent. The solution: you need to separate the angry feelings intended for your parent(s) from the feelings you have for your spouse. Ideally, your spouse should become an ally in this process by dialoguing with you. Here's how to do this:

1. Pretend that your parent is in the room.

2. Tell your spouse what you would say to your parent if he or she were present.

3. Identify what your partner does that reminds you of your abusive parent.

4. Finally, after you've realized what your partner is doing to upset you, tell your partner how this behavior reminds you of your parent.

In making this link, you achieve two ends: (1) your spouse will feel less personally blamed and more willing to listen to your pain and alter his behavior, and (2) discussing your pain with your loved one will help heal your Old Scar.

When verbal abuse has entered the relationship, it's always a good idea to seek professional help, because verbal abuse often leads to physical violence.

For B

If you are on the receiving end of verbal abuse, you must not reward your mate with any form of attention, which includes continuing to dialogue. When the verbal abuse begins, quietly and firmly say, "If you want to calmly describe what I said or did that upset you, I will listen. But if you continue to insult me, I will have to leave." If this limit doesn't work, you must walk away. If you have any fear whatsoever that limit setting will cause your mate to become more out of control, seek professional help at once.

Keep in mind that former victims are often afraid to stand up for themselves for fear of retaliation. If you have felt like a victim for a long time, professional help may be needed to help you break this cycle.

OLD SCAR #6

"Mommy and Daddy, please stop yelling at each other."

You or your mate grew up with parents who criticized, belittled, or put each other down.

How This Old Scar Often Surfaces
in Relationship Conflicts

Male or female: argumentative behavior

There will be very heated, unending arguments in which verbal abuse is present.

Type of Healing Needed

See recommendations for Old Scar #5.

OLD SCAR #7

"Daddy, don't hit Mommy."
"Mommy and Daddy, stop hitting each other."

How This Old Scar Often Surfaces
in Relationship Conflicts

Male or female: behaving abusively or becoming
the victim of abuse

When a person witnesses battering during the formative years, he or she may become a batterer or a victim of battering later in life. If physical abuse exists in your relationship, seek professional help at once.

OLD SCAR #8

"Mommy [Daddy], stop touching me that way."

How This Old Scar Often Surfaces
in Relationship Conflicts: A, B

(A) Male or female: *sexual shutdown*
You may feel sexually numb or experience a lack of sexual interest, which are protective mechanisms.

(B) Male or female: *sexual acting out*

If you were sexually abused as a child, you may become a sex addict, sexually unfaithful, promiscuous, or obsessed with kinky sex.

Type of Healing Needed

For A

If you feel sexually numb, Sensate Focus, described in these two paragraphs, is a good exercise to perform. The purpose of this exercise is to learn to enjoy the pleasure of being touched—without feeling pressured to become aroused. When memories and feelings associated with the earlier abuse arise, speak about this with your mate. Get out of bed (if you are there) and talk about the painful subject, as far from the bedroom as you can. You don't want to taint your bedroom with bad feelings about sex.

When you're being touched, make a conscious point of mentally separating your mate's touch from the abuser's touch. Repeat positive thoughts. For example, you might say: *My lover is touching me; It feels good; I want to be touched; I am entitled to have pleasure; My body is wonderful;* and so on. If this exercise doesn't succeed in resolving your problem, seek professional help.

For B

If you or your mate is sexually acting out, these behaviors are aimed at keeping the painful feelings away. You shouldn't be forced to abruptly arrest the troublesome sexual behaviors. They will diminish naturally as you are helped to face gradually the feelings associated with the earlier abuse and work them through. This type of work needs to be done in therapy.

OLD SCAR #9

"You like my sister [brother] more than me."

How This Old Scar Often Surfaces
in Relationship Conflicts

Male or female: feeling sided against

If you experienced sibling rivalry growing up, you may unconsciously arrange situations in which sides are taken. And as you know, relationship conflicts result whenever you think your partner is taking another person's side or doesn't agree with your point of view.

Type of Healing Needed

If you're on the receiving end of the setup, avoid getting backed into the side-taking corner. Give the emotional message that your mate is number one and that you're always on his side. And if you must take another person's side over your mate's, do not do it publicly. Make sure that you handle all issues where third parties are concerned when you're alone with your mate. If you must disagree, remember to preface your position with supportive statements and reminders that he is always number one.

For example, your mate wants the kids to go to bed early as a punishment, and you feel the punishment is too harsh. When you're alone together, this is what you might say:

> *You:* Honey, you know I think you're a great parent, but on this subject I think we need to reconsider. [You've started with a positive, supportive statement and then positioned yourself as part of his team.]
>
> *Your partner:* You're always taking their side over mine.
>
> *You:* I know it hurts you when I don't agree with you.
>
> *Your partner:* Yeah.
>
> *You:* Like when no one listened to your side and squashed you down. [Understanding goes a long way in showing you're on his side.]
>
> *Your partner:* Exactly.
>
> *You:* I understand how bad it was for you, and that's why we have to work together as a team to make sure the kids don't feel squashed the way you did.

It has not been my intention to lay blame on parents in this chapter. We all know that, despite their best intentions, parents make mistakes. You made mistakes, and so did your parents and their parents. These wounds pass from generation to generation. The point is that we all come to adulthood scarred in one way or another; and, as I hope I've shown, couples can do a great deal to help each other heal Old Scars by following my suggestions.

Let me remind you that awareness is the key to healing your Old Scars. By simply identifying what unresolved childhood issues are being re-created in your marital conflicts, and working together to resolve them, you are on the path to healing.

While marriage has the power to heal, we also know that most couples end up trapped in endless fighting cycles in which they relive, rather than heal, their childhood scars. During bitter fighting, many couples fall into endless, destructive communication potholes. In order to resolve conflicts, you must make sure that your mind is working for you, not against you.

♥ ♥ ♥

Chapter Six

HOW YOUR HEAD CAN BE YOUR OWN WORST ENEMY:

Training Your Mind to Fight For (Not Against) You

Misunderstandings are the source of many fights. As you will see, how you interpret your mate's actions or words will determine whether or not a fight breaks out. In other words, your head—that is, your interpretation of what you see and hear—can be your best friend or your worst enemy. It has been repeatedly shown that unhappy partners interpret each other's communications in distorted ways. And—you guessed it—the bias swings in the most negative direction possible. In this chapter, I will explain that negatively interpreting your mate is an ANS arousal trigger and the kiss of death to conflict resolution.

Why would a perfectly normal person read a partner in the most negative light? For one thing, Old Scars taint how you interpret the world. If you were spoken to in put-downs, you will expect to hear put-downs. If you were praised, you will expect praise. In other words, we hear what we expect to hear.

The Echo Process

Since we have chosen mates who resemble our parents, we unconsciously assume that they will relate to us the way our parents did. This leads us to distort the meaning of our mates' communications so that they fulfill our expectations. I call this the Echo Process.

In a very short time, the Echo Process takes a diabolical turn: our unconscious minds actually induce our partners to treat us in ways that are familiar to us. Let's use Lucy as an example. Lucy's father was critical of her, so we know that she'll be prone to hearing criticism in whatever her husband, Dan, says, whether or not the criticism was intended. Believing that criticism is coming at her all the time, she naturally responds to him in angry ways. Obviously, Dan feels angry to be falsely accused, and he begins to expect that every word out of Lucy's mouth will be an attack on him. Soon, he incorrectly reads even her most innocent statements as attacks, and everything he says comes out sounding angry and attacking, just like her father!

So you see, Lucy's mind has enticed Dan to treat her the way her father did. This is just what her mind wanted. But here's where most couples get stuck: History has repeated itself (Setting the Stage), and your partner treats you like your parent(s) did—but what about the Happy Ending? Instead of achieving a resolution to your early traumas, you feel nothing but resentment for each other.

What happens next in this atmosphere of chronic resentment? Since you're not getting love and support from your mate, you begin to engage in scorekeeping (*I'm right and you're wrong; I won and you lost*). Winning is an uplifting experience, and without knowing it, you're shoring up your ego, which isn't getting much support from your mate.

Unfortunately, this ego-boosting maneuver is relationship busting, because it sets up a deadly vicious cycle: it fosters more ANS arousal in men, which leads to more withdrawal, more anger on the wife's part, more disturbed chemistry and withdrawal, more anger on the woman's part, even greater disturbed chemistry, and more withdrawal.

Read the following conversation between Nancy and Phil, the couple we met in Chapter 5, and see if you can detect how the Echo Process has set off ANS arousal in Phil.

> *Phil:* Is tonight chicken night already?
>
> *Nancy:* Listen, if you don't like my cooking, make your own meals.
>
> *Phil:* I didn't say I didn't like it. I just couldn't believe that chicken night had rolled around . . . you know, how fast time flies. Why are you always overreacting? You're so hysterical.
>
> *Nancy:* Oh, here we go again, you're Mr. Perfect. You never do or say anything wrong.
>
> *Phil (rolling his eyes):* Oh God, my wife the hysteric.
>
> He leaves the room.

Nancy (shouting): I'd tell you to go to hell, but you're such a saint! Tell you what [dumping the food down the disposal], why don't you ask God to make your last supper?

What happened here? Nancy, hearing criticism in her partner's opening question ("Is tonight chicken night already?"), immediately attacked Phil. In turn, ANS arousal kicked in, and he became defensive and counterattacked, and then the fight (and the meal) went down the drain. This is where the relationship is going to end up if this couple doesn't learn to interpret each other's opening remarks properly, and stop fights before they start.

How can you train your brain not to steer you wrong? First, decide that for a trial period you won't immediately react when you feel criticized. This takes enormous willpower, but the payoff is saving your relationship. It's entirely up to you, and I promise you, the following technique has worked for the majority of couples I've treated. If you have decided to give this a try, read on.

How to Train Your Brain to Interpret Your Mate's Opening Statements Properly

Step 1: Hold Your Horses

The next time you feel that your partner's opening remark is a criticism or an attack, don't do or say anything. You may need a break, so tell your partner that you need a minute to work something out in your head. Leave the room if necessary.

Step 2: Take a Step Back in Time

Now, think back to your childhood. Ask yourself if your partner's remark reminds you of something from your past. Bring up any memory that seems pertinent. Who said what to you? What was that person's body language, tone of voice, and facial expression when he or she said whatever it was that upset you?

Step 3: Take a Hard Look at Reality

Ask yourself: *Were my mate's words, actions, body language, tone of voice, or facial expressions similar to the behavior of the person in my childhood memory? Is there any chance (even one percent) that there could be another explanation for his actions or words? Is it possible that I have misinterpreted him?* If you have the slightest question that there could be another, more positive interpretation, give your partner the benefit of the doubt.

Step 4: Check Out Your Suspicion

Now you can return to your partner and use a technique that I call the Check Out. No, I don't mean that you or your partner should check out of the relationship. I mean that since we decided there is the possibility that you may have been hearing your partner in an overly negative light, you need to Check Out your suspicion that you might be wrong.

Step 5: Smooth Any Ruffled Feathers
(Use as Needed)

This incident (your upset, your leaving the room) may have sparked ANS arousal in your partner, so make sure to smooth his ruffled feathers. To do this, you can tell him what the current incident reminded you of and explain that the intensity of your reaction stemmed from other issues. This technique is very effective in heading off ANS arousal and male withdrawal, because the focus of the blame is taken off of him and is redirected onto more neutral territory, such as your history.

How did Nancy and Phil put the five steps into practice? I'll show you how.

Replay of the Chicken-Delight Nightmare: I

Phil: Is tonight chicken night already?

Nancy: Honey, I'm having a reaction to that question. Give me a moment. [Hold Your Horses]

Nancy realizes that Phil's remark reminded her of her father, who always put her down. [Take a Step Back in Time]

Next, she reviews the vocal tone and body language that accompanied his statement and realized that they were neutral. [Take a Hard Look at Reality]

Now, she is ready to resume the conversation with him.

Nancy: I just want to be sure. Are you saying that you don't like my chicken? [Check Out Your Suspicion]

Phil (raising his voice): Of course not. Why do you always think I'm criticizing you?

Nancy: Honey, I understand you feel upset. Do you want to know why I misread you? [Smooth Any Ruffled Feathers]

Phil: Okay.

Nancy: You know how my dad always told me I couldn't do anything right? Well, I'm so used to being put down by him that I misinterpreted what you said. [Smooth Any Ruffled Feathers]

Phil: I get it now.

They hug and the misunderstanding is resolved.

With practice, you'll be able to perform steps one through three in the blink of an eye, and without leaving the room or interrupting the flow of conversation. When you reach this level of proficiency, you'll probably be able to move directly into the Check Out and skip the other steps. The following example shows what I mean.

Replay of the Chicken-Delight Nightmare: II

Phil: Is tonight chicken night already?

Nancy: I just want to be sure. Are you saying that you don't like my chicken? [Check Out Your Suspicion]

Phil: No, not at all—it's just that I'm surprised how time flies.

Nancy: You would tell me if you didn't like my chicken? [Check Out Your Suspicion again]

Phil: Yes, I would, and I do like your chicken.

Nancy: Which part of my meat do you prefer?
She giggles.

Phil: Well, you know I'm a breast man, but I also like the thighs, and especially the neck.

He walks closer.

Nancy: Are you hungry now?

Phil: I could do with a bite.

He takes her in his arms and nibbles her neck affectionately.

As you can see, by Nancy employing the Check Out technique, the opening remark was properly interpreted and a fight was avoided. Remember, fights are like railroad tracks: if you switch onto the wrong track, there will be a crash; but if you switch to the proper track (by correctly interpreting an opening remark), the crash can often be averted.

Excessive Personalization

In addition to negative distortions, chronically conflicted partners must weed out another type of cognitive distortion: excessive personalization.

Doreen's husband has been coming home late from work for the past few weeks. She automatically assumed that Leroy's behavior was directed at her (personalizing). Once Doreen began personalizing, her mind was off and running, concocting interpretations that tortured her half to death ("He's found another woman," "He doesn't find me attractive anymore"). When such ideas emerged, she felt hurt and angry. Next, Doreen acted out her anger (whining, complaining, criticizing, attacking), which triggered ANS arousal and withdrawal in her partner. His withdrawal, in turn, added fuel to her belief that he didn't love her anymore, and in no time, a major war was in progress.

While men find it hard to accept responsibility when they cause emotional pain, women are all too quick to personalize and hold themselves accountable when there is no reason to do so. For goodness' sake, and for the sake of your relationship, always assume that you are unnecessarily personalizing, and before becoming reactive, Check Out Your Suspicion to make sure that your perception is correct.

There are, of course, occasions in which a Check Out will confirm the accuracy of your interpretation. In such cases, you'll need to use the conflict-resolution techniques discussed in Chapters 8 through 10.

Once you've learned how to train your brain to fight for you, not against you, you're almost ready to sign a permanent peace treaty with your partner. But first, before any negotiation techniques can be acquired, you must learn the Climate Control.

♥ ♥ ♥

Chapter Seven

THE BATTLE-AX:

How Women Can Use Climate Control Techniques to End Relationship Fighting

Bernadette awoke in a sunny mood. Today was her day to lunch in her favorite café with her best friend, Sally. Her mood rapidly clouded when she tripped on her husband's dirty jeans, crumpled on the floor beside the bed. As she walked to the bathroom, she stumbled on a mine field of more dirty laundry. Inside the bathroom, she found a hairball in the sink and wet towels thrown inside the tub. Her anger began rising like mercury in a hot sun. She took a deep breath, slowly counted to ten, and headed for the kitchen, where she found the table littered with crumbs and coffee spills, the milk carton saluting her from the counter, and a pile of dirty dishes. Suddenly, her anger thermometer shot through the top. She yanked the phone from its cradle and pounded out Peter's office number.

He answered with a cheerful "Hello."

"You've done it again!" she shouted.

"What's your problem?"

"I'm not your freakin' maid, that's my problem. How many times have I asked you to clean up after yourself?"

"You're off the wall, you know that. Maybe you should see a shrink."

"You've got balls calling me a nut, you pig!" she shouted into a dead line.

Now Bernadette was in a very, very bad mood.

"Life's a bitch and then you marry one" is a saying that's plastered on truck bumpers across America. Where bumper stickers don't exist, you will probably find men huddled around campfires uttering complaints about the "Battle-Ax" who is back in her teepee stewing (and I don't mean tomatoes). I suspect that if people lived on the moon, we would find this slogan embroidered in the sky.

Many married women are angry over having to carry the bulk of domestic tasks, in addition to holding down outside jobs. The icing on the cake (that they baked from scratch) is the fact that their emotional needs aren't being met. And when a woman is upset, she makes sure her partner knows about it. Unfortunately, the expressive nature of the female gender role is the spark that ignites the physiologically hyperreactive male.

I'm not saying that you need to button it when it comes to issues that are troubling you. What I am saying is that before you can even think about tackling your relationship beefs, you must send ANS arousal and withdrawal behaviors packing. Otherwise you'll be attempting to negotiate with the back of your partner's head! Bottom line: before attempting to negotiate, you must first cool down the relationship climate with the following Relationship Climate Control techniques.

Relationship Climate Control: Create a Cool Climate by Meeting Your Mate's Needs

As I said in the Preface, anger and fighting are often the sad by-products of unmet needs. As you will discover, anger and fighting fade when you feed each other the right Relationship Essential Nutrients.

It's important to realize that the nutrients differ for men and women.

Relationship Essential Nutrients for a Man

Let's start with what a man needs from his partner.

Give Him Two A's

To simplify, the male gender role is instrumental and task-oriented, which means that a man focuses on actions and producing results. When a man loves a woman, he is wired to move heaven and earth to make her happy.

In turn, a man needs to feel that his woman values what he *does* for her. In short, men need to be Admired and Appreciated for their strength, power, and achievements, as well as their efforts to protect and provide for their women and offspring. These are the two *A*'s.

Most relationships go sour for men because women nag and complain about what their man is *not* doing right. In no time, a guy feels useless as a man, which causes him to give up on his partner and find another woman who does value him. Since couples tend to shower each other with praise during the honeymoon phase, it's easy for a man to feel seduced by the rewards of another new relationship in which he feels unconditionally appreciated. When a man gets appreciation from his partner, he doesn't need to go looking elsewhere for it.

To have a happy relationship or marriage, the savvy woman knows that she must directly state what she wants and what pleases her rather than complain after the fact over what she didn't get.

Now I know my women readers may be thinking: *If a man loves me, he should know what I want without my having to tell him!*

I'm here to tell you that nothing could be further from the truth.

Let me explain. Many people come to adult relationships dragging unhealed wounds from childhood. One common wound comes from having been raised by a mother who wasn't properly "attuned" to your needs when you were very young, a mother who wasn't sensitive enough to know what you needed when you were too young to speak your needs. If Mom didn't sense and meet your needs way back when, you will come to adulthood expecting your partner to guess your needs and fill in the blanks within yourself.

This wound is one of the many possible reasons why a woman might expect her man to read her mind and guess what she wants (or she may actually state the opposite of what she wants, expecting her partner to guess what she really means). She is looking for her partner to mother her the way her own mom should have.

Now hear me, and hear me good: *men are not wired to be mind readers.* No man on earth can be expected to make up for missing mothering. For one thing, they don't have breasts (unless they eat too much chicken!). Expecting them to pick up where Mother fell short is just a formula for failure.

You must get it through your head that expecting a man to read your mind is futile; it's just not part of his job description. So if you want to break the fighting cycle and create a relationship that works, you must directly state what you want.

But there's more. Remember we're talking about creating a positive feeling in a man by giving him the Relationship Essential Nutrients that he needs.

Well, when a woman says what she wants and her man responds to her needs, he must receive positive feedback from his woman (remember the two *A*'s: admiration and appreciation).

The smart woman knows that she must encourage a man to continue doing what works for her by *verbally* acknowledging and appreciating his efforts (women need the same consideration, of course!). This is simple conditioning. Think of Pavlov's dogs. Pavlov blew the whistle when he served food to his dogs, and soon the dogs associated the whistle with being fed. It didn't take long for the dogs to salivate at the mere sound of the whistle, even when no food was offered.

People are no different from dogs. When you feed (meaning *praise*) a behavior that you like, the person you praise is motivated to continue that behavior, since the behavior is associated with pleasure.

I know my female readers may be thinking at this point: *Why should I have to reward him for doing what he's supposed to do?* Well, think about how a baby learns to walk. He's supposed to walk, true, but he'll never learn how if his parents don't praise his efforts with smiles and cheers.

Grown-ups are no different.

Since all humans seek praise, when a woman offers adequate admiration and appreciation, she is fueling a man to continue doing what she likes. In fact, the praise that a woman offers her man is actually a gift that she gives to herself!

The point is, men will go to the ends of the earth and slay countless dragons to please the women they love. As long as a man feels that he is pleasing his woman, he'll never stop. When praise stops, a man loses all motivation to continue trying. What's the point if his efforts only fall on deaf ears or blind eyes?

Can you see the vicious cycle that occurs in many distressed relationships? A woman doesn't say what she wants. Then she nags and complains when her guy doesn't read her mind. He then feels hurt, angry, and unmotivated to do things for her. In turn, she becomes angrier and nags and complains even more, which makes him feel still more demoralized and unmotivated. Finally, he stops trying altogether, which fuels a downward spiral that ends in more fighting, cheating, and breakups.

Variety

In addition to admiration and appreciation, what else does a man need? As I said previously: variety!

Like most male animals, human males are biologically programmed to impregnate as many healthy females as possible in order to produce the largest number of offspring. This wiring ensures the survival of the species. In short, men are built for variety, not monogamy.

Choosing one woman goes against a man's biological programming. When a man does choose to settle down, or chooses to come back to a relationship, he must feel that his woman is so amazing that she possesses all the best aspects of every woman rolled into one. When he gets this feeling, he doesn't need multiple women because he feels that all women are embodied in the one he loves. When a woman is unpredictable and funny, and keeps her man guessing, she is actually fueling his need for excitement and variety.

When the craving for variety is satisfied within the relationship, most "normal" men are content to remain in a monogamous relationship (excluding the players, Don Juans, Casanovas, and commitment and intimacy phobics who can't be faithful due to their own emotional problems, buried rage toward women, or hidden homosexuality).

In addition to needing variety, men are also wired to choose the most desirable, healthy, and attractive females to ensure sturdy offspring. This explains why in both the animal and human kingdoms males compete against other males for the best females. In fact, men are wired to fight to the death in order to win a desirable female from other males who are also competing for her hand or rump!

Men are also drawn to a woman who conveys that she's smart and resourceful. On a primitive biological level, men know that these traits, when passed on, ensure the best offspring.

So remember, men are wired to move mountains and slay dragons in order to win desirable females away from other competing males. In turn, it's the woman's job to (1) praise her man's efforts, and (2) let him know that she's worth fighting to keep.

Relationship Essential Nutrients for a Woman

Now that we know what the Essential Nutrients for men are, it's time to discuss what women need to be happy in relationships.

If men are wired to be protectors and providers, a woman is biologically programmed to find a mate who will provide for and protect her and her offspring. Yes, it's that simple for a woman.

Don't be fooled. Even if a woman earns a good living and doesn't need a man to take care of her financially, her biological programming doesn't know this. This is why, as I said earlier, women choose life partners who are even more financially successful than they are. Women have a biologically programmed need to feel safe, protected, and secure. This need is fueled by a primitive, biologically based, survival-of-the-species imperative to choose men who will never abandon their women and offspring.

The need to be sure that a man will never abandon her and her offspring explains why a woman requires *frequent* reassurances in words and actions of her man's devotion. A woman needs to feel that she is first in her man's world, that he listens to her, takes her feelings to heart, and shows her in words and deeds that he values her above all others—all of which provide a deep feeling of security that he'll never leave.

Eight Basic Cool-Down Principles

Now that I've covered the Relationship Essential Nutrients, I want to discuss the eight basic principles for cooling the relationship climate.

Daily Bread: Maintaining the 5-to-1 Ratio

In happy relationships, couples maintain a 5-to-1 ratio of positive to negative communications. Social science researchers John Gottman and Nan Silver have found that for every one negative word, interaction, or communication delivered in a day, there are five loving messages offered to counterbalance the negative. If this ratio of five parts positive to one part negative is not maintained, a relationship quickly dissolves.

Distressed partners often tell me that their mates don't perform five praiseworthy acts in a year, let alone in a day. If you feel this way, I can assure you that your anger is blinding you from seeing the good before your eyes. Nursing your anger and refusing to see your mate's positive behaviors are a twisted form of self-protection. If you see the good, you might have to let down your guard and risk being hurt again. As long as you feel angry, you have your armor to protect you. But is all this anger really a protection? In the short run it may feel like it; ultimately, using anger as armor is destructive in that it sustains the war and prevents you from getting the love you need.

Try something with me. Don't let down your guard. Don't trust your mate. Even hold on to your feelings of anger, if you wish, but temporarily put them in your psychological bottom drawer. You can always pull the anger out of the drawer at any moment. Now, for the sake of your relationship, ask yourself, *If I weren't so angry, what could I praise in my partner's actions?* Write these things down.

Next, verbalize the praise to your mate. When you do, remember that you don't have to let down your guard or trust your mate. Just deliver the praise and watch what happens.

The Platinum Rule

Most distressed couples live according to the Golden Rule ("Do unto others as you would have them do unto you"). They behave as though they were attached to each other by umbilical cords and bestow on each other what they, themselves, want. For example, a wife who wants more nurturing may pour affection on her mate, who, in turn, may feel smothered by her acts of love. In such cases, neither partner is fulfilled. Here's another example.

> *Emily wants to be pampered when she is sick, while Aaron wants to be left alone when he's under the weather. Whenever Aaron is sick, Emily dotes on him, bringing him soup and medicine, secretly hoping that he will get the hint and pamper her when she's sick. All her fussing only annoys Aaron. Emily needs to stop giving Aaron what she needs and to start giving him what he needs, and vice versa.*

In happy relationships, spouses recognize each other's separateness, and live by the Platinum Rule: "Do unto the other mate what you know he or she wants."

The Team Comes Ahead of the Individual Players

Happy couples fight for the team, not for the individual players. They strive for a win/win situation, rather than a win/lose outcome. If either partner sees that a conflict isn't going well for the team, one or the other will yield, compromise, postpone discussions, or do whatever is needed for the team to win. This means that these couples systematically avoid the Fight Traps discussed in Chapter 3, all of which escalate conflict.

Knowing When to Shut Up

Happy couples know how to leave what's "better left unsaid" unsaid. In unhappy relationships, partners practice the "honesty is the best policy" approach. I don't know who is responsible for inventing that phrase, but without a doubt, it is the biggest fallacy ever to be foisted upon marriage. Don't misunderstand me. I'm not saying that you should lie. What I'm saying is that sometimes, saying *everything* can do more harm than good. I always tell my clients: "Before speaking, ask yourself, *If I say what I wish to say, will it be helpful to my mate and our relationship?* If your answer is *no*, then button it."

Knowing When to Let It Go and
When to Take It to the Mat

In unhappy relationships, every issue is considered a federal case. Tony Robbins calls this "majoring in minor things." Oftentimes distressed couples do this because unresolved issues and residual resentment (as well as disturbed body chemistry) are adding fuel to the fire. Before they know it, they're literally screaming over nothing.

Sometimes, making a federal case over small issues occurs because couples are—more or less consciously—trying to avoid discussing the real issues that are bothering them. Since they lack appropriate conflict-resolution skills, they know a fight will break out if they try to address the true problems. This avoidance leaves everyone edgy and prone to snapping over little things.

> *Sarah liked to think of herself as a forgiving person who didn't let little things get to her. Every time Steve left his shoes in the middle of the floor, she was annoyed, but didn't think such a petty thing was worth mentioning. When he criticized her cooking in front of his mother, she told herself (through clenched teeth) not to make a big deal over nothing. Then one night, Steve arrived home five minutes late for dinner, and Sarah, the queen of forgiveness, began screaming like a madwoman and flinging every piece of dinnerware across the room—winning the China Frisbee Champ of the Year award.*

Avoiding conflict discussions can blow up in your face. When anger is not discharged in the moment, an emotional residue, similar to soap scum, lingers, and that accumulated residue can foment an explosion when you least expect it. So when an issue is important, it must be addressed, not buried.

How do you know when an issue is important enough not to drop? I always tell my clients, "If it bothers you, it's important." If you tend to sweep all issues under your emotional rug, then assume, at least in the beginning, that everything is important. You will soon know what is and isn't worth getting riled about. Rule of thumb: deal with the issue promptly or let it go. But make sure that if and when you decide to let an issue go, you're not simply avoiding it and burying it in a shallow grave.

Knowing When to Call a Permanent Truce on Certain Topics

Happy couples avoid discussions of hot topics that have no bearing on the relationship (for example, political differences). Unhappy couples, by contrast, have a habit of returning to their areas of difference, forever trying to impose their opinions on each other. When this is done, all that gets imposed are bad feelings.

Giving the Benefit of the Doubt

I have spoken often about how your mind can be your own worst enemy by assigning a negative slant to your mate's communications. The technical term for this is *mind reading with negative effect,* and unhappy couples have Ph.D.'s in this one. Happy couples, by contrast, give the benefit of the doubt to their mates, assuming the best, not the worst, possible interpretation of their mates' words, actions, and gestures. This positive bias sets an upbeat tone to the relationship so that a self-fulfilling prophecy occurs. When you expect to hear positives, these are the types of communications you invite. Keep practicing the Check Out Your Suspicion exercise in Chapter 6, which will teach you how to give your mate the benefit of the doubt—a vital relationship-climate cooler.

Red Alert:
Recognizing Relationship Danger Zones

Happy couples are experts at recognizing their Relationship Danger Zones (physical or emotional exhaustion, illness, loss or death of a relative or friend, or having been angered in the recent past) and making sure to avoid important discussions until one or both of the partners is less vulnerable.

General Cool-Down Techniques for When Conflict Strikes

In addition to the eight cool-down basics, you need to know how to cool the climate when either of you is hot under the collar.

Keep a Calm Tone

Gottman and Silver also found that unhappy couples can be distinguished from happy couples by the tone of voice they use when speaking with each other. Chronically conflicted couples speak to each other in harsh, whining, sarcastic, and irritable tones, whereas happy couples never speak to each other in these ways. Did unhappy couples develop these harsh tones after they became unhappy, or did these harsh tones contribute to their unhappiness? Who knows? What we *do* know is that if you don't drop your guns and ammunition, you'll never end your skirmishes. To find out if harsh tones are reverberating in your house, why not conduct an experiment? The next time you and your mate have a conflict discussion, turn on a voice recorder. Try to forget that it's running and speak naturally. Then listen to yourselves afterward. Honestly examine how you both sound. I bet you'll be surprised. To quote from the poem "To a Louse" by Robert Burns: "O wad some Power the giftie gie us to see oursels as ithers see us!" In order to achieve relationship harmony, we must amend the quote in the following way: "To hear ourselves as others hear us."

Requests vs. Reproaches

When a woman hurls reproaches at her partner, he doesn't know how to translate her complaints into a request for behavioral change. Take a look at some of the complaints that many women utter:

> *"You don't love me anymore."*
> *"There's no romance anymore."*
> *"Your work is more important than I am."*
> *"I'm not special to you any longer."*

Can you see how these complaints leave a man clueless? He knows that he is accused of failing in some way, but such reproaches leave him in the dark. Instead of criticizing and complaining to your partner about what he does *not* do, you must learn to *directly* ask for what you need, *before* he has the chance to let you down. Make it a request instead of a reproach.

Again and again I have heard unhappy women swear to me that they have clearly told their partners what they need and that their partners simply refuse to respond. Those same blank-faced men swear that they have never heard their wives or girlfriends tell them what they want from them. Is someone lying? The woman has said what's bothering her, and she has said it over and over. So, why hasn't her partner heard her?

The answer to the mystery lies in the fact that *most women complain bitterly and forcefully about what they're not getting from their partners.* In the face of heated complaints, a man falls into ANS arousal and his brain shuts off. He can't hear or process communications, so it turns out he wasn't lying when he said that he never heard what his wife or girlfriend wanted. The man's lack of hearing makes a woman turn up the volume on her complaints. Big mistake, because, as you know, raising the emotional level further cranks up a man's ANS arousal, and turns him stone-deaf. Take, for example, Mike and Erica.

> For years Erica raged over her husband's coming home late, his avoiding her by hiding out in the basement, and his not sharing in household tasks. She cried to me in session that he didn't care for her. I asked her if she had ever explained to her husband how his behavior made her feel. She swore up and down that she'd repeatedly told him over the years.
>
> We decided to meet with her husband. Mike skulked into the session, like a kid on the brink of a scolding. He sat on my couch and stared at the carpet.

Erica told him that she was through with him. She was tired of his lack of responsiveness.

I asked her to stop her tirade and calmly describe his behavior and the effect it had on her.

She persisted that telling him was useless.

I told her even if it was useless, to do so anyway. And this is when the miracle occurred.

She calmly and clearly described the behavior that was troubling her and reported how it made her feel.

Mike suddenly broke into tears and said that he had no idea what he was doing to her. He said that he loved her and would change his behavior. They sobbed in each other's arms and connected for the first time in over a decade.

The upshot of the story is that, thanks to Erica's cool presentation, Mike finally heard her, and he changed his behavior. The couple ended treatment with me soon after. Bad for business, but good for the marriage!

Because of past failed attempts, you may be skeptical or afraid to hope that your partner could actually respond to you. Let's run a little experiment. Directly tell your mate what you want. In order to protect yourself from disappointment, assume that he won't respond. I think you'll be surprised by his willingness to respond, assuming that you have a mate who wants a relationship with you and isn't too riddled with Old Scars.

Timing

Knowing when to approach your mate is an important trick for keeping a conflict discussion cool. I have often observed that women in unhappy relationships have a knack for approaching their partners at the world's worst times. For example, one of my patients, Suzie, always cornered her husband for their serious discussions when he was glued to the television set, ready for the big play. It's no surprise that he was ready for the wide receiver, not to receive *her*. It so happened that Suzie's unconscious mind was playing a nasty trick on her by guiding her to approach him precisely when he wasn't available, in order to replay her old abandonment scar! Becoming aware of this self-damaging pattern freed her to break the pattern and approach him when he was receptive to her. The point to remember is: if your mate seems tired, irritable, or preoccupied, abort your mission and wait for another time.

In order to get out of the habit of picking wrong times, you need to "Knock Before Entering" instead of crashing into your mate like a Mack truck. (I will thoroughly discuss this skill in Chapter 10.) The point to keep in mind is that Knocking is a simple process in which you ask your mate, "Is now a good time?" or "Do you have a minute?" These sentences show your consideration for your mate and foster a more receptive response. Knocking also models for your mate how he must use consideration when approaching you.

Wait Until the Dust Has Settled

Don't approach your mate in the heat of the moment. Until you are more effective at handling your conflicts, you're in danger of losing your cool and resorting to Fight Traps. So take five, or however long you need, to analyze what is happening for you. Privately examine what Old Scars have been torn open by your current conflict.

Know When to Call Back the Troops

When a discussion seems to be cycling out of control, women in happy relationships know how to do one of two things: abort for a later time, as I mentioned earlier, or use the methods outlined in this chapter to cool the climate down.

Humor

Research shows that anger and humor cannot coexist because the biochemicals that accompany humor are incompatible with those that accompany anger. Humor is best directed as oneself or at a situation, and should never come at the other mate's expense. In the following example, humor was used to deflate a situation that could easily have caught fire.

Beth and Leon were visiting his sisters in Europe. Beth was much younger than Leon, and his eldest sister never missed an opportunity to belittle her in a foreign language that sounded like alphabet soup to Beth. On one occasion, her sister-in-law pulled a high chair to the table and motioned for Beth to take her seat. Beth was fuming, but not being fluent in her sister-in-law's language, she had no choice but to swallow her feelings. Later, when she was alone with Leon, she told him how she felt about his not telling his sister that she was out of line.

"I was very angry at you for not sticking up for me."

"I should have. Honest to God, I was so caught up in my conversation with Enrique that I didn't see or

hear what she did. What do you expect from such an old husband? I'm practically blind and deaf."

"Very funny. Okay, since you're so old and I'm so young, how about I arrive for breakfast in Pampers tomorrow?"

"And I'll roll in with my wheelchair."

Just Say No to Sarcasm

Humor should not be confused with sarcasm—a potent Fight Trap that occurs when a person pretends to agree when he really doesn't. Sarcasm can also take the form of cutting remarks. If you want to achieve relationship harmony, all forms of sarcasm must be eliminated. Let's replay the dialogue of our couple on European holiday and show how easily their humor could have dissolved into sarcasm.

"What happened to your mouth back there?"
"What do you mean?"
"Why didn't you stick up for me? How ball-less can you be?"
"You know how ball-less I am. You've been wearing mine for years."

In addition to the previous techniques for troubled times, you will also need to master the following techniques, which will help you ensure a cool climate all the time.

Acceptance of Differences

In happy relationships, both partners are willing to tolerate differences on many levels. In unhappy unions, divergent opinions and attitudes are taken as personal insults. In order for a marriage to thrive, partners must be secure enough to recognize and allow each other to exist as separate beings.

It's vital that partners tolerate each other's feelings and emotions as well, which rarely happens in distressed relationships.

Don't Mind Read

On a related note, since men are accustomed to taking matters into their own hands, they often assume what their partners want and need, and then act upon their assumptions, without checking. These assumptions can easily lead to broken hearts.

When Blain and Tamara separated, Tamara moved back in with her parents. The couple visited each other on weekends, hoping to achieve reconciliation. For weeks Blain faithfully visited his wife—until he learned that, after their visits, his mother-in-law harped on her daughter about how much she disliked him.

In order to spare his wife the pain of her mother's nagging, he stopped visiting. His pulling back was his way of caring for his wife. Only one problem: she didn't want him to stop visiting, and felt rejected by his withdrawal.

Distressed partners get into trouble when they assume what their mates think, feel, and need, and then act upon these assumptions. The spouse on the receiving end of these "gifts" often feels wiped out and rejected. So in consideration of your mutual separateness, and in order to avoid relationship distress, never assume what your mate needs. Always check.

No Unilateral Decisions

One way to turn the relationship climate into the sweltering tropics is to make decisions that affect your partner without mutual discussion. Make sure that you talk over every plan, big and small, before making it a reality.

Paul and Claire had accumulated $40,000 in savings. One day, without consulting with Claire, Paul emptied the savings account in exchange for a 380 Mercedes. He was floored to find that his wife was in tears. "But Paul," she sobbed, "you just blew the down payment for our house."

Remember the Weekly Special

In addition to the broad suggestion that couples maintain a 5-to-1 ratio of positive-to-negative communications, my research has shown that, in order to feel loved, a woman requires frequent reminders that she is special to her husband.

Husbands often tell me, "I show her that she's special. I come home on time. I don't cheat. I give her my paycheck." In response, wives say, "Every good husband contributes in this way to his family. It's an obligation. A duty. I need to know what is special about me. Why you care for me instead of someone else." In short, women need regular reminders that they are as special to their partners today as they were in the first days of their relationship.

Giving flowers and chocolates has become the industry-standard way of showing wives and girlfriends that they are loved. The only problem with flowers and chocolates is their universality (all men give them) and, hence, some women feel that a husband who bears flowers is performing a ritual rather than expressing a true feeling of love. This predicament can be easily solved: simply communicate to your mate what actions or gestures he can perform that would make you feel special—a phone call, a massage, a weekly date, buying you a piece of jewelry, preparing your favorite meal.

You may be thinking, *But I've told him a thousand times what I want.* I must remind you that most women make two fatal mistakes: they either complain over what they're *not* receiving, thereby rendering their partners deaf and unresponsive; or they make general rather than specific requests, such as "Treat me special," instead of saying, "I would feel special if you would surprise me with a new dress."

Believe me when I tell you that if you clearly communicate your needs, without being vague or critical, a loving partner will usually respond favorably.

The men I've worked with have found it helpful when their partners create a Weekly Special list from which they can freely choose. The key word here is *freely:* men must feel free to choose how they will demonstrate their love to their partners. So the list must not read like a series of commands.

It's also important for men to understand that women feel loved and cherished when their partners initiate loving gestures without having to be prodded. If a woman feels that she must beg, plead, or remind her mate to deliver the Weekly Special, she will feel deeply hurt or burning mad. Since the only burning we want to see is the flames of love, remember that the Weekly Specials need to be initiated from the heart and without reminders.

Hamburger Helpers

For those of you who are unfamiliar with Hamburger Helper, it's a packaged food product designed to turn minute quantities of leftover meat into a complete meal, thereby making a little go a long way. One day, the idea struck me: women need relational Hamburger Helpers. That is, in addition to the Weekly Special, which is a loving action, women need regular verbal reminders that they are near and dear to their men's hearts.

Don't Forget His Pat on the Back

In order to help your mate respond to your needs without being nagged, a pat on the back is highly effective. Never forget that while women need to be reminded that they are special, men need verbal reminders that their efforts are appreciated. So, make sure to let your mate know that you value his efforts to respond to your needs, and tell him every day.

Conveying Emotional Understanding

The feeling of being understood (perceived understanding) is considered by some marital researchers to be the most important element in a happy relationship. It's an especially difficult skill for men to acquire, since they think in action-oriented terms and find it hard to believe that understanding alone is often all that's required. The best way to teach this skill is through gentle guidance during a discussion. The following is an example of how to do this.

> *Ethel:* My sister was so mean to me. What did I ever do to her?
>
> *Jim:* I have a good mind to call her up and set her straight. [fixing, action-oriented]
>
> *Ethel:* I know you mean to be helpful, but what would help me most right now is your simply listening to how I feel. [gentle guidance]
>
> *Jim:* What good is that? I think you'd feel better if you called her back and gave her a piece of your mind. [fixing, action-oriented]
>
> *Ethel:* Honey, I know you want to fix this for me. Just understanding how I feel is all the fixing I need. [again, gentle guidance]
>
> *Jim:* You mean if I listen to you and understand, you'll be happy?
>
> *Ethel:* That's all I need.

Keeping Promises

Broken promises are hurtful and damaging to a relationship. When a partner habitually breaks promises, we can suspect that a passive-aggressive personality disorder—in which anger is expressed indirectly by breaking promises or withholding—is operating. Broken promises can also result from a dependent personality disorder. The dependent partner will make promises that he doesn't wish to keep, simply to appease the other spouse or avoid the other's anger. When broken promises are caused by character disorders, professional help is needed.

There are also occasions in which broken promises are not caused by personality disorders. For example, men often follow a course of action that they think will please their partners, and in so doing, they often forget or override previously made promises. It has been observed that men find it difficult to simultaneously pursue two courses of action.

> *Louis had promised to take Tina to dinner to celebrate their tenth anniversary. Earlier that week, Tina found a house that she fell in love with. From that moment on, Louis made it his sole priority to find a way to buy her that house (goal-oriented), and he spent every waking hour looking for a way to finance it. Unfortunately, he forgot that he had invited his wife for a dinner date. When the time of the date came and went, Tina was crushed that he had forgotten her. From Louis's point of view, he was thinking of Tina, and only Tina, but this obliterated from his memory his scheduled dinner date with her.*
>
> *Tina found some solace in understanding the way Louis's brain is wired. He forgot their dinner date because his brain had a hard time simultaneously processing the two imperatives, the house purchase and the dinner.*

Broken promises damage trust and erode relationships. It's important to do whatever is needed to follow through on commitments.

Verbal Embraces

When a man finds it impossible to respond in action to his partner's request, he can still respond with verbal open arms. I always use the following example to demonstrate my point.

> Judy was in a jewelry store admiring a diamond ring. She said to her husband, Kurt, "I love that ring so much . . . I wish you could buy it for me." Kurt, in turn, responded in a negative fashion by saying, "What are you, crazy? You know we can't afford that ring." This response crushed Judy, and not because he couldn't or wouldn't buy the ring, but because he didn't convey the <u>feeling</u> that he would have loved to buy the ring—if he had the money. By saying, "I would love to buy it for you. It would look so beautiful on you. I'm so sad that I can't afford to give it to you now. As soon as I can, you know I will," he would be conveying his desire to say yes to her feeling or wish, even though he couldn't respond in action.

Saying yes to a woman's desires is often just as fulfilling as consummating the wish.

Seeing the World from Your Mate's Point of View: Partial Identification

The Cool-Down techniques described previously will remain a cumbersome list of directives that are easily forgotten unless you develop Partial Identification—that is, a place in your heart and mind for your partner. Partial Identification is nothing more than knowing how to keep one foot on your mate's emotional side of the fence. No relationship can thrive without it.

I do not suggest that you forget who you are and become a clone of your partner. That would be Total Identification. Total Identification is sometimes experienced when two or more people obtain absolute similarity of opinion or feelings. This state may occur during a concert or at a religious ceremony of unusual intensity. Total Identification is not always a plus. It occurred during the political rallies organized by the Nazis, when participants experienced such enthusiasm that their individuality disappeared in the common excitement.

Partners, at times, can also reach nearly Total Identification—also called Merger. In these cases, the separateness of each person disappears and the couple lives under the illusion that they are in total agreement on ideas, opinions, and emotions. For some couples, this merger is an ongoing experience. For others, it's only transitory: during great sex or while strolling together on a moonlit ocean boardwalk. These privileged moments of fusion are efficient ways of maintaining and re-creating the unity of the marriage. Although these moments may create the illusion of permanent and total unity, such accord does not exist as a perpetual reality. The sense of oneness is broken when daily activities intrude, underscoring separateness and differences. And when this illusion of unity is broken, conflict often develops.

Some couples experience conflict because they constantly live in a state of Merger. Merger leads to attempted mind reading, and when this occurs, partners believe that they know what the other needs, wishes, or feels, and invariably fail to recognize each other as separate beings; hence, they are inattentive to each other's real needs.

What is desirable in marriage is the conscious joining of two people who, in spite of their differences, work to combine these differences through mutual understanding. This unity of two different people is the achievement that causes both partners to feel that their individuality is acknowledged, respected, and understood. It is reached through Partial Identification, which means that you remain yourself and stay in touch with your own needs and agendas, but make space in your heart and mind for your mate's needs and feelings.

Partial Identification and Similarity

Partial Identification is easiest to achieve when the two interacting people are similar—when they share the same culture, life experiences, values, or moral codes. Twins can readily identify with each other. Similarity of gender also helps. We all know the camaraderie that exists among soldiers, club members, fathers, husbands, and so on. Similarly, women have their cliques, clubs, and coffee klatches.

More difficult is Partial Identification with members of the opposite sex, even when they share much in common in terms of culture, social class, or religion. This is why spouses commonly complain about the opposite sex. In the musical *My Fair Lady*, professor Henry Higgins exclaims: "Why can't a woman be more like a man?" And women, sipping their coffee, make fun of their obtuse husbands who do not grasp the simplest aspects of female psychology.

The difficulty in understanding someone of the opposite sex is usually compounded by other differences (ethnic origin, religion, cultural background, social status, tastes, interests, and so on). In spite of all these differences, people who desire a happy relationship must work at understanding each other—that is, they must Partially Identify with each other.

Interestingly, when you're engrossed in a book, play, or movie, you often actively identify with the characters, which can help you better understand yourself and your mate. But obviously, you also need to discover your partner directly to determine how you both are similar and how you differ. Daily dialogue, mutual openness, and patient description of points of view are necessary to discover what feelings each of you experiences in given moments.

This basic groundwork is necessary and must be undertaken before any conflict or tension can be successfully addressed. If you practice Partial Identification during moments of calm, the skill will be firmly under your psychological belt when you need it most: when conflict erupts. But make no mistake: no matter how much you have practiced, when trouble hits, you'll find it very difficult to Partially Identify. However challenging it may be when you're confronted by your partner, you must temporarily put between parentheses your own ideas, opinions, or emotions, and make space in your mind and heart for those of your partner. If you succeed, your Partial Identification will express itself in sentences like "I see what you mean" or "Yes, I can understand that you felt *x, y,* or *z* when I did this [or said that]."

For the process to be successful, you must resist the temptation to defend yourself; you must also be willing to accept responsibility for the fact that your behavior or words have created discomfort, pain, hurt, or anger in your mate.

In order to understand what your mate feels and take responsibility for your part in creating that pain, you must be sufficiently secure in your worth. You must possess a solid self-esteem.

Partial Identification and Globally Negative Statements

To help yourself accept your relational shortcomings, yet another condition must be met. You must realize that it's not possible for your partner to accept and identify with globally negative statements. This is why global accusations, insults, and name-calling (Fight Traps) are the enemies of relationship happiness. For example, "You did it again," "You'll always be the same bastard [or the same bitch]," and "You never show me love and respect" are all difficult to accept due to their global quality. Expecting the attacked partner to identify with these across-the-board condemnations would be tantamount to requesting that person commit psychological suicide.

Similarly, the attacked partner may be tempted to use sarcastic self-deprecations under the pretext of identifying with his angry mate ("Yes, you're right, I'm an abominable husband. Yes, I understand, I'm a beast, utterly stupid, an SOB," and so on). When such sarcastic answers are made to an accusing partner, they cannot be sincere or express any form of identification because no one in his right mind could identify with such statements about himself.

In order for the confronted partner to Partially Identify with his mate's statements or feelings, the confrontation must be limited to a specific aspect of behavior. For example, a statement like "When you used the word x, y, or z, I felt very hurt" is an acceptable confrontation that permits the confronted partner—through further questioning—to understand the feelings that his or her behavior created.

In essence, it's the responsibility of the confronting partner to construct a precise and focused description of the problem and to present it coolly. In so doing, the person on the receiving end will find it easier to Partially Identify with what is being said.

You also need to realize that Partial Identification must be employed by both partners in order for a successful conflict discussion to occur. The confronting partner has two tasks: he or she must speak in a way that the mate can tolerate, and must also be able to Partially Identify with his or her mate's reactions to the confrontation. And the confronted partner must Partially Identify with the feelings that his or her mate presents. So, as you can see, each partner needs to Partially Identify with the other.

Exercises to Partially Identify with Your Mate's Feelings

How can you learn to Partially Identify with your mate? You both must open your hearts to each other and tap into your feelings of love. I can't stress this point enough: love is the key that unlocks your heart and permits you to Partially Identify with each other.

How can you access feelings of love when you're angry? A good way to do so is to recall those special moments together, those rare periods of Total Identification that I spoke of before. You may recall a particularly excellent sexual encounter; you might choose to recall one of your partner's qualities that you especially love. Whatever works for you.

Exercise 1:
Switching Roles

In addition to accessing your feelings of love, another way to perfect your Partial Identification skills is to temporarily switch roles. Select an area of conflict and play your mate's position, and vice versa. Make sure to play your roles believably. Feel the way you know your mate feels; state your mate's position. If you've played your part well, you'll have an easier time empathizing with your mate's emotions. And if you make the effort to mentally switch roles when conflicts arise in the future, you'll be taking a giant step toward resolution.

Exercise 2:
Find the Same Feeling Within Yourself

Sometimes, it's difficult to Partially Identify because you're having a hard time relating to why your mate feels the way he does. To get around this, forget the situation that triggered his feelings, and instead, recall an instance in which you felt what he feels. Once you have the feelings in mind, you can more easily understand your mate, even if you can't relate to the specific event that triggered his emotions.

♡

By applying the various Cool-Down and Partial Identification techniques described in this chapter, you will abort your partner's ANS arousal and withdrawal behaviors. The result of this is a mate who sticks around to resolve conflicts with you.

Now that you know how to cool the relationship climate, you're ready to move into the second part of the book, which will show you how to resolve your conflicts. The first chapter in this section outlines the one skill that is the bedrock of conflict resolution: listening.

♥ ♥ ♥

Chapter Eight

LISTENING TO THE BATTLE CRY:

How to Use Your Ears to Resolve Conflicts

On the road to conflict resolution, listening is the superhighway. To be heard is no idle need; it is deeply healing to the soul and the mortar of a happy relationship. This explains why women in unhappy relationships most frequently complain that their partners are unable to properly hear and respond to their emotions.

In this chapter, I present the Listening Blunders, the enemies of good listening that must be avoided at all costs, and outline the Listening Blocks that cause them. I also describe the five basic listening skills and show you how to teach your partner to be a good listener.

Why Is Listening So Necessary?

Each time there is a social unit of more than one person, it's essential that the parties properly communicate. And, of course, no communication is possible without mutual listening. To be happily united, partners must learn a special kind of communication—*emotional communication*—and a type of listening—*listening to the emotions.* While you must listen to your boyfriend's or husband's emotions in order to prevent ANS arousal, it's perhaps even more important that your partner learn to listen to yours. This is because relationship satisfaction is highly correlated to a *man's* ability to listen to his partner.

Feeling heard and understood is so vital to a woman's relationship satisfaction that there is actually a technical term for it: *Perceived Understanding.* As a consequence, this chapter will concentrate on the type of listening that is most crucial to relationship satisfaction: listening to each other's emotions and, more particularly, teaching your partner to listen to yours.

Because your partner has not been trained to listen to emotional communications, he will need to do the lion's share of learning. Being less skilled than you puts him in a one-down position, which is a hard place for a man to find himself. So be sensitive to his feelings of vulnerability and be careful not to make him feel patronized.

Also keep in mind that you and your mate may become frustrated over the time required to master listening skills. When you're ready to give up, remember that emotional listening is not something that can be learned overnight— so don't put a stopwatch on the listening learning curve. You must keep practicing the exercises contained in this chapter in order to reap the benefits. Listening skills take time to acquire.

Listening Blunders

Before I show you the various listening skills, you must first identify and eliminate the Listening Blunders that occur when listeners unwittingly drop their mates as a result of in-attention and/or a lack of knowledge as to how one should respond. In all cases, the Listening Blunders have the universal effect of breaking the emotional connection.

Don't Hang Up—I'm Still Talking

In Don't Hang Up, the listener ends the conversation without checking to be sure that the speaker is finished. This makes the speaker feel emotionally dropped.

> *Yvonne:* I was so sad today.
> *Hank:* What about?
> *Yvonne:* My friend Sara is moving to Texas next fall.
> *Hank:* That's a bitch. What's for dinner?

In the above example, Hank started out with a bang, but ended with "dinner." Many listeners forget to make sure that their partners are finished before they "hang up" the discussion. A simple "Are you finished?" or "Would you like to stay with this a little more?" or "Can we move on?" is all that's required.

I'll Get Back to You

In I'll Get Back to You, the listener drops the speaker with the intention of returning to the topic. Unfortunately, the speaker has no way of knowing that the listener will ever return to it, at least not in this century.

> *Denise:* I was aggravated today when your mother called and told me off.
>
> *Frank:* What about?
>
> *Denise:* She said that I should be spending more time at home with you and the kids.
>
> *Frank:* It's really none of her business. Which reminds me—my boss's line was tapped and they taped him propositioning a hooker. Can you believe it?
>
> *Denise:* What does that have to do with what we were talking about?
>
> *Frank:* I was going to come back to it, but when you mentioned Mom's phone call, it reminded me of the boss.

In the above example, Frank broke focus with Denise, leaving her to feel dropped and unheard. A listener should never shift the topic of discussion before the speaker is finished. If this must be done, then it should be done explicitly (like call waiting), so that the speaker knows that the listener will be returning.

Changing the Subject

Changing the Subject occurs when the listener abruptly shifts the topic of discussion.

Kathy: The bus was late today.
Neil: My boss was sick.

While Changing the Subject can reflect inattention or a skill deficit, it can also have the effect of breaking an emotional connection.

You're Sucking Me Dry

This Listening Blunder occurs when the listener makes a self-referential, disconnected response to the speaker's emotional communication. For instance, a wife says to her husband, "I just remembered our anniversary celebration, and a wave of love came over me." To which the husband might reply, "Yes, I felt so happy that day." This answer is an emotional remembrance, not an emotional response. By referring to his own inner feelings and not linking back to his wife (for example, he could have said, "I still feel the same love for you"), she will feel emotionally dropped.

Another, subtler example of a self-referential response is the following. A wife says, "I have very loving feelings toward you," and the husband replies, "What you just said makes *me* feel very happy." At first glance, the response provides the illusion of connection because the husband made an explicit reference to his wife using the word *you.* But his sentence only addressed his own contentment. Like a child, the husband is happy because his "mommy" has fed him emotionally. But where does this leave the wife? With chafed nipples!

What was missing in this husband's response was an emotional communication that echoed his wife's feeling statement. Something like "I feel happy and close to *you* when *you* tell me that" is just what the marriage doctor ordered!

Changing Emotional Levels

Changing Emotional Levels is a gross form of dismissal that occurs when the listener shifts the conversation away from an emotional content. It occurs regularly in intimate relationships and invariably leads to conflict. I discuss the reasons why many men Change Emotional Levels under the heading "Fear of Intimacy" in the next section on Listening Blocks. For now, let me simply show you some examples of Changing Emotional Levels.

In the following example, Burt Changes Emotional Levels with an abrupt escape.

> *Anne:* I feel so happy that you're my husband.
> *Burt:* Thanks. How many years have we been married? I need to know for the insurance.

Instead of an abrupt escape, a person can use subtler tactics to avoid an emotional connection.

> *Jeff and Donna are getting dressed for a night out with friends. Donna catches a glimpse of her husband knotting a necktie he hasn't worn since their honeymoon. "Oh Jeff," she says. "I remember the first time you wore that tie. We were dancing at the Lido di Venezia. I can still feel your arms around me. Just looking at you wearing it makes me feel so much love for you."*

A subtle way to blow off such an emotional connection would be for Jeff to offer an intellectual comment: "Yes, it's an old tie. The type of pattern they used in the '90s."

Jeff could also avoid connection by saying, "Yes, it's a nice tie. Do you remember where you bought it?" In this case, there is a seeming connection—the recognition that the tie was a gift from Donna—but the connection is factual, not emotional.

Not Leading with the Feeling

Not Leading with the Feeling occurs when the listener provides an unemotional response to the speaker's feeling statement.

Laura—an attractive blonde whose blue eyes were as pink as an albino rabbit's, thanks to nonstop crying—was desperate because she could never connect with her husband. Every time she made a feeling statement, he answered by talking about stocks. She discussed the matter with him and thought he had understood.

"But last Saturday night was another example," she said. "The kids were away at the sitter's house and we were at our favorite restaurant, Chez Marcel. It was very romantic—candlelight, soft music. . . . Anyway, I could tell women were giving David the eye. He looked so cute. So I smiled at him and said, 'You look so handsome tonight. You're getting me turned on.' And then he did what he always does. He started talking about his office and my heart turned to ice. I wanted to crawl in a corner and die."

When Laura confronted David, he answered, "I was about to tell you that just today a client saw your photo in my office and said how pretty you are."

As you can see, David's heart was in the right place, but his words were in the wrong order. He didn't lead with a feeling statement, which would have connected him to Laura.

Rushing in with Solutions

Offering practical solutions is another way of bypassing a woman's emotional communications. When a man jumps to offer solutions, he means to convey that he understands his partner's problem; unfortunately, the opposite is achieved, and the woman feels emotionally dropped. In order for a woman to feel heard, her partner must verbally convey that he understands her feelings and leave it at that. See the section on Male Listening Blocks, under the heading "The Doer Freaks," to understand the cause of this blunder.

Cheer Up

When a man tells his upset girlfriend or wife to Cheer Up, she feels stifled and angry. This angry reaction totally bewilders men. (*Why is she so mad? I'm trying to comfort her.*) If your partner employs the Cheer Up blunder, he needs to be told that if he wants to cheer you up for real, he must ride out the storm with you—meaning, accept your feelings and stay on your emotional level for as long as you need.

What Causes Listening Blunders?

Now that you're familiar with the various types of Listening Blunders, you need to understand and resolve their causes.

The Blunders of Inattention, which occur when the listener is preoccupied, can be due to three different factors: *skills deficits, intense preoccupation,* and *fear of asserting oneself.*

When Listening Blunders are due to skills deficits, they can be easily remedied by becoming aware of the blunder and practicing a better response.

If intense preoccupation is causing the Listening Blunders, you both will need to become more aware of your inner states so that you can directly communicate when you're unavailable to listen, rather than listen with half an ear. What's more, the speaker can protect herself from being on the receiving end of this type of blunder by making sure that her mate is available to listen to her before she launches into an emotional discussion.

The third cause of Blunders of Inattention can be due to what I call the Unentitled Citizen Syndrome. In such cases, the listener is afraid to assert himself and tell his partner that he's not available for discussion, so he will pretend to listen, saying, "Uh-huh, yeah . . . " while continuing to pursue his own line of thought. In the process, he may commit any or all of the Listening Blunders. Before someone can be a good listener, he must first entitle himself to defer a discussion politely when he isn't 100 percent available to listen.

The Blunders of Inattention generally aren't the result of deep-seated Listening Blocks. However, the second type of Listening Blunders—refusal or avoidance of emotional connection—can be caused by various types of blocks, which I will discuss in detail below. Keep in mind that some Listening Blocks are unique to men, others to women, and some are shared by both sexes. I'll begin by discussing the Listening Blocks that are common to both sexes.

Listening Blocks:
Discomfort Over One's Own Feelings

If a person is unable to tolerate the strong feelings that are induced by the speaker's communication, it will be impossible to listen and properly respond.

The first three Listening Blocks—*Poor Self-Control, Applying Laws of Morality to Feelings,* and *Applying Laws of Logic to Feelings*—all stem from the discomfort that arises when strong feelings are discussed. These Blocks all involve an unconscious attempt to push down intolerable feelings.

Poor Self-Control

Listening automatically stirs feelings in the listener. When a person believes that all feelings must be acted upon, the only way to guard against going out of control is to avoid feelings and the listening that triggers them. Sexual and aggressive impulses are particularly threatening because of the consequences that would result if they were to be enacted. That's why I call these two impulses the Dynamic Duo.

Theresa entered my office hanging her head in shame. She told me that she could never divulge to me what she was feeling because I wouldn't like her anymore. I wrote down on a piece of paper all the "horrible" feelings I could imagine and asked her to circle all that applied. Big surprise—sex and anger were circled.

Why couldn't Theresa openly admit to her feelings? Because she feared that her behavior wasn't fully under control. If she felt like axing her husband or having sex with the mailman, then she must act out that feeling, right? Wrong. You can think and feel whatever you want, so long as you know that you can separate thoughts and feelings from actions. Once you've got it straight, feelings lose all their power. Until this Block is resolved, it will be impossible for you and your mate to listen to each other's feelings.

Applying Laws of Morality to Feelings

When someone feels that it is morally wrong to harbor negative feelings, that person will indict him- or herself whenever unacceptable feelings surface and shut down or refuse to hear communications that trigger such feelings. The person suffering from this problem will often be heard saying, "I [You] shouldn't feel that way" or "I [You] have no right to feel that way."

Condemnation of feelings makes it hard for either partner to stay on his or her mate's emotional level, in which case listening will go out the window.

Concepts such as "right" or "wrong" have no place in the emotional realm. Feelings cannot be squelched by moral preaching.

Applying Laws of Logic to Feelings

Many people try to reason away their feelings ("It doesn't make sense to feel the way I do"). Since feelings are as irrational as the wind, applying laws of logic to the emotional realm is an exercise in futility. Imagine saying to the wind, "It would be better if you blew from the opposite direction"! In order to be good listeners, both partners must be able to accept all their feelings.

Inability to Identify with Your Mate

Another Listening Block occurs when your mate finds it impossible to understand how and why you feel the way you do. When this occurs, your mate is having trouble identifying with you. And in this case, the tendency is to pull away emotionally or to say things like "I don't understand why you're so upset." Obviously, these remarks let the speaker know, loud and clear, that her mate isn't able to hear her.

If either partner struggles to identify with the other, refer again to the Partial Identification exercises, which are thoroughly described in the previous chapter.

Fear of Intimacy

Since the listening process creates a close bond, if a person is terrified to be too close, that person will have a tendency to tune out emotionally laden communications. Fear of intimacy often conceals a fear of dependency, abandonment, engulfment (self-annihilation), and more. Refer to Chapter 5 on Old Scars in order to find out how to heal these wounds. Until these Old Scars are resolved, Listening Blocks will continue.

Male Listening Blocks

Feeling Responsible

As I've said before, since men feel responsible for their partners' well-being, when a woman is upset, her mate tends to feel guilty. In order to assuage his guilt, he will attempt to fix the problem by trying to talk her out of her painful feelings (the Cheer Up Listening Blunder). When a man is engaged in this operation, listening goes down the drain.

The Doer Freaks

Since men have been socialized to be fixers, not feelers, they find it hard to stew in the emotional juice with their wives. For them, any conversation about feelings is a waste of energy and time—meaning the conversation needs to end as soon as possible. As a consequence, men will pull out their psychic toolboxes and try to fix their partners' problems with the only gadgets they have: rationalization, intellectualization, and, most of all, problem solving. These men do to their partners exactly what they have been trained to do for themselves—to reroute their feelings into the intellectual and practical realms, where they can be extinguished by solutions. This rerouting, of course, takes them miles away from listening.

You can turn your partner's practical and logical tendencies to your advantage and to the advantage of your relationship by methodically teaching him the various tasks and skills associated with effective listening. In this way, his productive side will be satisfied.

The Macho Defense

Many men are terrified to let down their macho guard, fearing that their maleness will be lost. (They feel that their sexual apparatus may shrivel and fall off if they're not acting like "real men" every minute.) Sitting with a woman who feels upset forces a man to confront his own feelings of vulnerability. To help your Wimp Phobic get around this block, remind him that "it takes a tough man to make a tender . . . listener."

Female Listening Blocks

When your partner is finally willing to acquire listening skills, you may discover mind-sets in yourself that threaten to jam the wheels of progress.

Fear

In Chapter 2, I explained that many fears keep us from moving ahead. No one is telling you to give up your fear, but it would be best to move forward in action (listen to your partner), despite the feeling.

Anger

If you've felt unheard for a long time, you may be resistant to listening to your mate. ("He never listened to me, so why should I listen to him?") Acting on this feeling is an emotional payback—a Fight Trap—that you need to abandon.

To soften your resentment, remind yourself why your partner hasn't been listening to you—he's been in chronic ANS arousal. This should help you to extinguish your resentment and start listening to him. When you listen, you will be heard in turn, and your anger will soon subside.

Also keep in mind that holding on to your anger will interfere with your partner's listening abilities. If you're seething with rage, you risk communicating inappropriately. In order to be heard, you must make sure to communicate a message that's "hearable." This means that your verbal communications must not be attacking or critical; otherwise ANS arousal and withdrawal reactions will be triggered in your mate, the very reactions that interfere with his listening abilities.

When I speak of a message that's hearable, I'm referring to more than overt verbal content. Recent studies have shown that nonverbal behavior can also trigger ANS arousal and withdrawal behaviors in men who are in distressed relationships. Nonverbal behaviors include body language (facial and bodily expressions), gestures, and vocal tones. Keep in mind that a mean look or a harsh or whining tone of voice is all that's required to set off that downward chemical spiral that leads to male withdrawal. So it's entirely up to you whether or not you will speak and behave in a way that makes your mate want to unplug his ears.

I Won't Praise Him

If you want your partner to learn to listen to you, you need to praise his efforts. Many women greet this suggestion with the enthusiasm reserved for a dental cleaning. They often tell me, "He should have known how to listen all along." And where was he supposed to learn listening skills? In school? From his father?

Why is it that women freely encourage and praise their girlfriends as they make strides along the path of self-development, but are reluctant to praise their husbands' learning efforts? There are several reasons for this. The first one is chronic resentment. When you feel angry, words of praise don't naturally fall from your lips. But there's a deeper reason for the reluctance. It stems from the belief that a husband should know what you need without your having to tell him what you want, let alone praise him.

To explain where this expectation comes from, we need to understand the preverbal stage of childhood. Since a young child cannot speak, he or she requires a parent who is capable of sensing every need. It's great if the parent succeeds in properly guessing. If the parent doesn't, which is usually the case, the child is left with a craving for a correction. Cut to 20 years later: we marry, and our unconscious minds see a second chance to receive the emotional goodies we weren't fortunate enough to receive as kids. This explains why, when a wife is furious that her husband doesn't magically know what she needs, she is really saying, "My mother should have guessed what I needed and you owe it to me to make up for my earlier losses."

Heaven knows it's hard enough for a biological mother to guess correctly each and every time. How on earth can a husband, a male who was never trained to be emotionally tuned in, be expected to guess? But this is what many wives expect. When their husbands don't guess, or guess wrong, or don't even realize there is something to guess, they are furious. So, when a woman refuses to praise her mate, she is actually thinking, *He didn't give me what I want, so to heck with giving him praise.* Talk about shooting yourself in the emotional foot.

In order to get past this impasse, you must remind yourself that your mate cannot be a mind reader. What's more, humans cannot acquire new behaviors if praise is withheld. When you praise his efforts, he'll be motivated to engage in the hard work necessary to learn the listening skills that speak to your heart. So you will actually be doing yourself the favor.

♡

Now that you've identified your Listening Blunders and and are working on resolving the Blocks that cause them, you're ready to learn how to listen.

Listening Defined

As you embark on your emotional listening crash course, the first thing you need to know is that listening is an active process that requires two separate tasks: (1) *clarifying* that the speaker's statements have been accurately perceived, and (2) *verbally conveying* to the speaker that the delivered message has been heard and understood.

I emphasize the word *verbally* because it's common for a man to silently reflect on his partner's communications, but offer no response. As far as a woman is concerned, she might as well be talking to a gerbil. In truth, many men, if asked to do so, could probably accurately restate the essence of their partners' communications (presuming they aren't in cognitive shutdown). But a woman doesn't know that her partner "got it" unless he tells her so. I cannot stress strongly enough that effective listening is actually effective *responding*.

Listening Skills Translated into a Man's Language

Since men are most at ease in the logical and practical realms, their willingness to acquire listening skills increases when they are presented as task-oriented steps. Nearly every husband or boyfriend who has followed my program has learned to listen and respond to his wife or girlfriend's emotional communications. As Karl told me, "I always loved Gina, but now I have the tools to listen, and she finally feels how much I love her."

Put a Sock in It and Just Listen

In order for you to teach your mate to listen to your feelings, he must get the idea that he needs to put a sock in it when it comes to offering unsolicited advice or solutions. Of course, you can't tell him in these words, but you can tell him, in concrete terms, exactly what you do need from him. When I say to be concrete, I mean spell out exactly what you expect from him. Remember, only psychics know how to read minds, so if you need him to listen and stow the solutions, then tell him.

Dottie, like many women, assumed that her husband knew that she needed him to simply listen to her when she was upset. So, when Russell gave her advice instead, she figured he was just being a withholding bastard. (Remember how our minds can be our own worst enemies.) By believing this, Dottie set herself and her husband up for war. Whenever her husband pulled out the advice, she pulled out her weapons of destruction. Not surprisingly, when she started firing, he had no idea why. When Dottie was finally able to tell Russell, in concrete terms, that he should skip the advice and simply listen, he started to get the picture.

Based upon my research with all types of couples, the following phrase most effectively gets the "put a sock in it" point across: "I know you mean to be helpful with the advice, but what would really help me is if you would just listen and understand what I'm feeling."

Becoming a Good Listener: Five Basic Skills

There are five basic skills that people who are successful listeners employ in combination. These are *Mirroring, Restating, Asking for More, Questioning to Clarify,* and *Staying on the Same Emotional Level.*

Mirroring is nothing more than reflecting back exactly what the other person has said. This technique shows that a person is listening.

Restating is a form of Mirroring in which the speaker's message is reworded slightly.

Asking for More is a technique in which the listener draws out additional information.

Questioning to Clarify ensures that the listener has thoroughly understood the speaker. This questioning process serves two purposes: it clears up any confusion that may exist, and it shows that the listener is actively listening.

Staying on the Same Emotional Level helps the speaker feel psychologically held, heard, and understood.

Let's start with Mirroring.

Mirroring

In this exercise, choose a subject that is bothering you, but make sure to avoid your hot topics. We don't want intense emotions to interfere with learning the technique. Now, *coolly* discuss *one* feeling that has been aroused in you as a result of your conflict. It is your partner's job to mirror back the feeling that you present. When his Mirroring is accurate, you will say, "Yes." If his Mirroring is inaccurate, try again until he succeeds. Then, move on to your next feeling. It's a good idea for the listener who is Mirroring to use a questioning vocal inflection. In this way, he leaves room for you, the speaker, to clarify in the event of misunderstanding. Use the following dialogue between Amy and Ken as an example of how you can practice Mirroring.

> *Amy:* I can't believe that my boss didn't say hello to me today.
> *Ken:* You can't believe that he didn't say hello?
> *Amy:* Yes. And it really hurt my feelings.
> *Ken:* Your feelings were really hurt?
> *Amy:* Yes. And I even felt a little nervous that my job may be on the line.
> *Ken:* You're worried that your job may be on the line?
> *Amy:* Yes.

You get the idea. This exercise is driving home a technique that good listeners use automatically. Whenever a person's words are mirrored back, it creates the feeling of being truly heard.

Restating

In the next exercise, Mirroring is elaborated upon through Restating. This is an excellent skill because the speaker knows that someone is making an attempt to understand, rather than just mimicking, which, if used to excess, can make the speaker feel like she is talking with Polly the parrot.

> *Amy:* I can't believe that my boss didn't say hello to me today.
> *Ken:* You were surprised, weren't you?
> *Amy:* Yes. And it really hurt my feelings.
> *Ken:* Besides surprised, you felt hurt, too?
> *Amy:* Yes. And I even felt a little nervous that my job may be on the line.
> *Ken:* So, you were surprised, hurt, and nervous all at the same time?
> *Amy:* Yes.

Asking for More

Asking for More information serves a clarifying function and conveys that someone is making an active attempt to understand. This technique is achieved by combining interested body language (raised eyebrows, wide eyes, and nods) with questions like "And?" or "And then what happened?" The following passage shows how it works. The best way to teach your partner this technique is for you to demonstrate it for him.

> *Liz:* You know, my sister was really nasty today.
> *Gene:* What did she do this time?
> *Liz:* It was the tone of her voice. She was really snotty.
> *Gene (leaning closer, eyes widening):* What did she say?
> *Liz:* She told me that because I hadn't been working for a while, I wouldn't understand the competitiveness in her office.
> *Gene:* And what did you say?
> *Liz:* I told her that I was offended.
> *Gene:* And then what happened?

I think you can see how effective this technique is in conveying interest in all the details of a mate's communication.

Questioning to Clarify

Researchers have found that happy couples live in harmony because the men in these relationships possess excellent encoding skills—meaning that they accurately interpret what their partners say. Make no mistake: good encoders are not psychics by birth. In fact, these men probably are as much in the dark as distressed boyfriends and husbands when it comes to understanding what their partners mean when they speak. So how does a happily united man manage to interpret his partner properly? It happens through a questioning process. Developing this takes practice, but it's worth the effort to learn it. This is an essential listening skill. The following dialogue shows how Questioning to Clarify looks.

> *Pauline:* You know, I can't believe that you were late for dinner so many times this week!
>
> *Tim:* Are you saying that you're angry with me about it?
>
> *Pauline:* Well, I am angry, but I don't think that I'm angry with you.
>
> *Tim:* Well, then who are you angry with?
>
> *Pauline:* I'm pissed with that job of yours.
>
> *Tim:* That job is putting food on the table!
>
> *Pauline:* I think that you're feeling attacked by me.
>
> *Tim:* Yeah. I was starting to get a little hot.
>
> *Pauline:* Let me start over. I appreciate what a good provider you are. I'm just annoyed that your boss makes you work late so often.
>
> *Tim:* So, you're pissed at my boss?
>
> *Pauline:* Yes. And I wanted you to just understand that when you're not here, I really miss you.
>
> *Tim:* So, you miss me, eh?
>
> *Pauline:* That's it, mainly. And I hope that your boss hires the assistant he promised soon.
>
> *Tim:* I miss you, too, you know. Anything else?
>
> *Pauline:* Come home earlier as soon as you can!
>
> *Tim:* You know that I will. And I understand how hard it is on you and the kids.

To develop the Questioning to Clarify skill, deliver a feeling statement and have your mate ask five clarifying questions. For example:

> *Opening statement:* I was really upset today.

Question 1: Did I do something? [Questioning rather than jumping to conclusions]

Clarifying statement: Not at all.

Question 2: If it wasn't me, then who upset you?

Clarifying statement: I really need a few minutes to calm down.

Question 3: Are you telling me to leave you alone? [Not jumping to conclusions. Checking before acting upon a potentially wrong interpretation.]

Clarifying statement: No, don't go. Maybe you could give me a hug and comfort me.

Question 4: Sure. When you say, "and comfort me" . . . is there something besides the hug that would comfort you?

Clarifying statement: Yeah, a massage would be nice after a hug.

Question 5: A massage and a hug, and that's it?

Clarifying statement: That would be great.

Had the husband in the above example not asked the five clarifying questions, he could have easily misinterpreted his wife's communication. What's worse, misinterpretations often turn to disaster because many husbands act upon their false assumptions. I can't stress enough the relationship-saving importance of learning the Questioning to Clarify process along with the Five Questions technique.

Looping Back Until Consensus Is Reached

If the Questioning to Clarify process were to be diagrammed, it would appear as large loops, and loops within loops. The loops indicate questions, clarification, restatements, and more requests for clarification. This process is continued until "perceptual consensus," or a meeting of the minds, is reached. Here is an example of Looping Back:

> *Bob:* I'm really sick of these family vacations.
>
> *Sue:* Are you saying that you don't want to vacation with my family anymore?
>
> *Bob:* I wouldn't go that far. It would be nice if we didn't vacation with your family every summer.
>
> *Sue:* So you don't want to vacation with them every summer?
>
> *Bob:* Right. Maybe every other summer would be better.
>
> *Sue:* So it sounds like every other summer would suit you. But I'm wondering . . . since you said "Maybe," are you not entirely sure?
>
> *Bob:* It's true. I'm not sure. If it's okay with you, can we leave it open and talk about it when next summer rolls around?
>
> *Sue:* Okay. We'll discuss it next summer.

Staying on the Same Emotional Level

Staying on the Same Emotional Level is a listening skill that is the exact opposite of the Listening Blunder called Changing Emotional Levels. Staying on the Same Emotional Level means that, for the duration of your listening process, you consciously become the Siamese twin of your mate. As such, you don't try to pull left or right; to do so would create psychological injury similar to the tearing that would occur if you tried to pull the twins apart. Staying on the same emotional level is a form of Partial Identification.

The best way to teach your spouse how to stay on your emotional level is to warn him before you begin speaking that the communication you're about to deliver is of an emotional nature. By alerting him before the discussion begins, you'll help to abort his natural tendency to shift the conversation away from feelings and onto solutions. It's preferable to put him in the right frame of mind before the talk begins, rather than wait until he fails. Reproaching him for his failure to stay on your level is the best way to trigger ANS arousal, which will make it impossible for him to listen to you in any form.

Ten Minutes a Day Keeps the Marriage Counselor Away: Part I

Now that you and your partner are familiar with basic listening skills, what comes next? Let's start with ten minutes of One-to-One Time per day, in which you take the time to listen to each other. At first, you should be the only speaker, and your partner the listener. I say this because it's too overwhelming for a man to learn to listen to his partner and disclose his own feelings at the same time. After your mate has successfully mastered the skill of listening to your feelings, you can include another ten minutes for him to discuss his own, if he wishes. Don't be surprised, however, if he isn't chomping at the bit to disclose feelings about issues that are bothering him. Most men prefer to concentrate on solutions that they devise on their own. So your partner may want to spend his ten minutes explaining how he resolved a problem.

Before you begin your ten-minute One-to-One Time, remind your partner that he is to listen and not offer advice or try to talk you out of your feelings.

Keep It Light for Starters

Don't begin by discussing the topics that concern your partner's behavior toward you. They are too hot, and until you've learned how to properly handle these delicate subjects (discussed in the following chapters), you must practice in more neutral territory. It will be much easier for your mate to listen to you when he doesn't feel personally responsible for having caused your ill feelings. So for starters, discuss an issue that has nothing to do with him at all. Once he is able to hear your feelings on a neutral subject and has some successes under his belt, then you can move into deeper relationship waters. Examples of subjects to start with: someone who annoyed you at work, on the road, or at the bank; your best friend; your boss; your mother, father, sister, or brother. I repeat: stay away from your mate and the relationship.

Time and Place

Set a time and a place for your One-to-One Time. The only way that this "date" can be broken is if one of you is dead! Also, remember not to have this discussion in the bedroom. I don't want you to associate heavy conversations with the bedroom. Heavy breathing, yes; heavy conversations, no.

Strokes

After you've completed your discussion and your mate has succeeded in listening, praise him to the hilt. Remember that it's human nature to want to repeat pleasurable experiences. If your mate recalls that your talk time was positive and that he succeeded, he'll be ready to take on the next listening challenge.

And don't be too discouraged if you had to remind your mate to keep his advice on hold; reminders are normal in the beginning. In any case, your mate deserves praise for hanging in there and trying to listen.

Ten Minutes a Day Keeps the Marriage Counselor Away: Part II

After your partner has managed to listen and stay cool during several ten-minute rounds, you're ready to discuss a relationship issue that is upsetting you. Since I don't want intense emotions to gum the works, please save the hottest relationship topics for later, after you've mastered the techniques in the chapters to come. Above all, avoid issues that are close to your mate's ego, such as sexual performance or anything else that you know to be a hot topic.

In fact, while you're learning the listening skills, I suggest that you discuss a make-believe problem. If you and your mate are hard-core realists and must discuss actual conflicts, make sure to present neutral issues (for example, behaviors that are upsetting you but that can be easily remedied). Only you can say what qualifies as a relatively neutral issue for both of you.

The listening skills that I've discussed in this chapter are the bedrock of successful relationship communication. When practicing your listening skills, it would be helpful for you to conceptualize the skills as notes in a musical scale. By artfully blending the various notes, you, too, can compose relationship harmony.

While I focused in this chapter on helping boyfriends and husbands build listening skills, you also need to perfect yours. As you read the next chapters, you'll see that listening skills are required at each phase of conflict resolution. If you don't listen to your partner, your discussions will derail long before you see a resolution. Only keen listening will enable you to recognize when a discussion is heading in the wrong direction, bring it back on track, and see it through to resolution.

♥ ♥ ♥

Chapter Nine

ON FURLOUGH:

Knowing When Not to Negotiate

Before you learn to negotiate, you need to know that in many instances, negotiation is not required and may even be inadvisable. I know you may be thinking that I'm complicating matters. But in the end, I will actually be saving you a lot of headaches.

Many relationship manuals and therapists are quick to advise distressed couples to negotiate because it's a structured process that yields observable results (when successful). But there is another reason why people are quick to negotiate: it helps them to avoid feelings.

We all know how uncomfortable emotions can be, and so it feels easier to negotiate a contract—an agreement that outlines behavioral change—and steer clear of emotionally rough seas. In the short run, everyone feels better, but in the long run, the tide of emotions swells even higher. This is because the overt issues have been negotiated, but the underlying emotions still churn beneath the surface. And when this happens, your negotiations will fail and you will feel even angrier than before.

There are other reasons why negotiations may fail: you may be negotiating nonnegotiable issues. There are three classes of issues that are nonnegotiable: violations of what I call *Relationship Laws, Emotional States,* and *Value Conflicts.* Let's examine these in detail.

Violations of Relationship Laws

There are basic requirements that must be met in order for a relationship to survive, and whatever people think or say, if these are not obeyed, there is no relationship. Here is a list of these violations:

- Degrading language, name-calling, sarcastic put-downs

- Physical abuse of the partner or the children

- Sexual abuse (partner or spousal rape, sexual abuse of the children)

- Infidelity (unless both partners have agreed to an open relationship or marriage)

- Alcoholism/drug abuse

- Irresponsible spending behavior or gambling that endangers the welfare of the family or impinges on the other partner's needs

- Refusal to discuss and arrive at agreements regarding parental practices

- Refusal to work (job or housework) and equitably support the family

- Systematic refusal to consider partner or spouse's feelings and to work at understanding them (for example: "That's the way it is. If you don't like it, the door is right there.")

If you are the object of any of the above behaviors, you must put your foot down and state that they are unacceptable. A mate's systematic and repeated refusal to change is cause for separation, not negotiation.

At this extreme point, couples often make one last-ditch effort and schedule an appointment with a marriage counselor. However, the rigid disposition of either of the partners may render this effort dead on arrival.

Emotional States

Emotions that are triggered by your mate's actions or words are the second class of nonnegotiable issues. Let's say you feel hurt that your husband forgot your birthday this year. How can you negotiate about being hurt? The birthday has passed. All that is left are your feelings, which need to be heard and understood, not negotiated. I insist on this point because many couples will try to negotiate their feelings away.

> *Ron:* Susie, you know life would be easier if you didn't get so angry each time I make a joke about your weight.
> *Susie:* Are you trying to tell me I shouldn't feel the way I do?

Ron: Yeah, kind of. I'd be more willing to work around the house if you didn't get so upset with me.

While you can negotiate about behaviors that upset you, the feelings that arise out of your mate's upsetting behavior cannot be negotiated or bartered away. So, when dealing with your own emotional states, the best way of operating is to disclose your feelings, and for your mate to listen and understand, using the techniques discussed in the last chapter.

A good way to help your mate understand your reaction to his words or actions is to use the Should I Be Feeling . . . ? technique. This technique helps a fragile or defensive partner discover the effect that he has had on you, without your having to point the finger at him. For example, you and your mate are discussing a subject—the content doesn't matter—when suddenly he blurts out, "You don't know what you're talking about." Your feelings are wounded, and you need to help him understand how his words landed with you. Obviously, you can't negotiate a contract about your emotional reaction to his words. And if you blast him outright for his inappropriate behavior, he will probably become defensive and tune you out. Here's where the Should I Be Feeling . . . ? Technique comes in handy. You say, "Should I be feeling . . ." and then you insert your emotion—whatever it may be. In the case of the above example, you would ask, "Should I be feeling put down?"

The advantage of this technique is that it helps your mate discover the impact of his behavior (enhances his Partial Identification) without getting his back up. Be aware, however, that some highly defensive mates could respond to the formula by saying, "Feel however you want to feel.

Your reaction has nothing to do with me." In such instances, the mate is refusing to look at himself and accept responsibility for the effect of his words or actions; in these cases, you will need to use a variant of the above technique, and instead of saying, "Should I be feeling *x*?" you'll say, "How do want me to feel when you talk to me that way?" This question forces the other person to take a look at his behavior.

Not only are your emotional states nonnegotiable, but the same holds true for those of your partner. Again, I have to distinguish between feelings and actions or reactions. That is, if your mate acts on his feelings and behaves inappropriately, that behavior can be negotiated. But the feelings themselves—that is, the raw emotions—are not subject for negotiation.

> *Eleanor's husband, Michael, often freezes up when she approaches him for an emotional connection. On one such occasion, she put her arms around him and told him that she had just remembered one of their first dates, in which they danced cheek to cheek at an elegant nightclub. Michael was silent and unresponsive and stared into space. Eleanor was crushed and fled the room in tears.*

Why did Michael freeze up? To find out, Eleanor needs to approach Michael and explore the origin of his reaction. In doing so, she will discover that his action-oriented brain had mistakenly translated her communication into a request that he do something concrete—to take her to the club in the near future. Michael knew that they didn't have the money for a night out, and he became immobilized by the fear of disappointing her.

In a situation like this, there is no place for negotiation. Michael can't negotiate on fear, and he can't negotiate about his wrong interpretation of his wife's request (thinking that she wants to go dancing) because this has nothing to do with what she expects of him—an emotional connection. Negotiating about dancing would play into Michael's action-oriented tendency, and it wouldn't address what the conflict is about: the fear that was aroused in him when he mistakenly translated her request for connection into a request for action. What Michael actually needs is to take his focus off of actions, and learn to talk about his own feelings and respond to his wife's feelings.

Interpretive Contracts

Even though your partner's emotional states cannot be negotiated, you may find it helpful to negotiate what is called an *Interpretive Contract.* This is an oral contract that focuses on the circumstances that may give rise to intense emotions and/or cooperating with your partner to abort particularly severe emotional reactions. With this type of contract, one partner is given permission to point out—without recrimination—troublesome or hurtful behaviors when they occur, or to spark a mate's awareness before a habitual reaction has the chance to occur.

For example, Eleanor and Michael's Interpretive Contract might be the following: Michael gives Eleanor permission to warn him before she attempts to make an emotional connection (to head off a freeze-up). She will also remind him that no actions (or expenditures) are linked to her upcoming approach, to help him take the focus off of action. And Michael agrees to clarify the nature of her request, in order to do what he can to head off his immobilizing fear. The discussion that is inherent to an Interpretive Contract will teach Michael to be less action oriented because when thoughts and feelings are put into words, they are much less likely to be enacted. And what's more, the intense emotions that cause him to freeze up will also diminish, thanks to the cathartic nature of the talking process.

If you and your partner decide to engage in an Interpretive Contract, there are two points to keep in mind:

1. You must make sure that your partner consents to having his frailties pointed out. Without his consent, you risk offending him, which will only trigger ANS arousal and you'll be back to square one again.

2. When you spark your partner's awareness, you must do so in a loving way. He must get the feeling that you're working on this problem as a team. If, at any point, your mate feels mocked or belittled, this technique will prove ineffective and even counterproductive.

Value Conflicts

Value Conflicts are the third type of nonnegotiable issues. When I speak of values, I'm referring to religious, cultural, and political beliefs; tastes; preferences; and so on. These values make up the core of an individual and are not up for negotiation. To attempt to do so would be like trying to force a leopard to change its spots.

There is much to be said for homogamy—or similarity—of values in intimate relationships. In fact, homogamy is highly correlated with relationship satisfaction: there is little friction, since the couple already sees eye to eye. Couples who are less homogamous, but still get along, have learned to either accept their differences or steer clear of conflictual subjects.

Unfortunately, many distressed couples are in trouble because they're fighting and negotiating about Value Conflicts without knowing it. For example, you and your mate have different preferences regarding where you like to have sex: your mate wants sex on the living-room floor, whereas the Beautyrest mattress is as wild as you like to get. Neither person's preferred location is wrong. Each of you is entitled to his or her tastes.

On the subject of tastes, let's discuss Vicky, whose bathtub drain is clogged beyond belief with an outsize hairball. "If only Pete would outgrow his hippie phase and buzz saw that mound of spaghetti on his head, I wouldn't be forced to play Mrs. Plumber," she lamented to me. She went on to explain that Pete likes his hair long and refuses to cut it, and they habitually argue on this subject.

Is this a negotiable issue? It's about Pete's hair values, and either Vicky can live with them or she can't. However, if Pete's long hair impinges on her by clogging the drain, then she may have a subject worthy of negotiation.

♡

We have spoken so far about the fact that attitudes, tastes, and preferences are nonnegotiable, but what about habits? If habits are value laden, then they are also nonnegotiable. For example, each Saturday morning, you like to dive into the household chores, but during that time, your husband has a habit of lounging on the couch, avoiding anything productive. You may feel tempted to negotiate for a change of behavior. But what if your husband's habit is value laden? Let's say he was raised an Orthodox Jew and was prohibited to do any work on the Sabbath. In this case, relaxing on Saturday mornings is part of his value system.

Here's another example. A husband has a habit of paying the bills at the very last minute. He was raised by parents who were hippies. They believed that life should be primarily fun and filled with freedom, and that work and chores could be done whenever. So as you can see, this husband's habit of paying bills in the eleventh hour is also value laden.

Now, if his wife was raised in a family that taught her to be early for appointments and deadlines, then her expectation that the bills be paid early is also value laden. In this case, the couple has a clash of values. What can be done about this?

Since values are an integral part of a person's makeup, you can't ask someone to negotiate away a part of his identity any more than you can be asked to do this. Demanding that your partner alter a behavior that is value laden is like asking him to commit psychological suicide. What's more, expecting someone to relinquish a value-laden behavior is tantamount to saying that his value is wrong and yours is right. This type of qualitative judgment doesn't apply to values. Values may clash, but they can't be labeled wrong or right.

So how can you deal with a Value Conflict? You have three options:

1. Ask yourself, *Do I really want to get into a war over this value-laden habit?* Asking this

question may lead you to simply accept your differences.

2. You can address the Value Conflict as though it were an emotional issue by listening to each other's points of view, without trying to enforce a behavioral change on each other.

3. As a result of your mutual understanding and respect for each other's values, you may decide to negotiate a resolution that is acceptable to both of you, one in which both of your values are respected. To do this, follow the negotiation steps outlined in the next chapter.

When dealing with habits that annoy you, it would be wise to ask yourself, *Is this habit directed against me?* Since women are prone to excessive personalization, you need to beware of the tendency to wrongly assume that your partner is hanging on to a habit to intentionally annoy, provoke, or defy you. Ask yourself, *Would my mate still engage in this annoying habit if he lived alone? Did he act this way before I was on the scene?* Very often, when you examine the issue with a cool eye, you'll realize that the habit is not directed against you. This may help you to let the issue go.

Sometimes, Value Conflicts are smoke screens for deeper issues.

Paula and Jerry continually argue about whether or not to marry. He believes that love is all that counts and that a piece of paper is not needed to prove his love. Paula wants a lavish wedding bash.

These two people share different values on the subject of marriage. Either they can decide to live with their differences or they can't. But there also may be more going on here than meets the eye. Maybe Paula and Jerry are fighting about "I do" or "I don't" instead of facing deeper issues. Perhaps arguing about whether or not to marry conceals deep fears of intimacy and commitment.

Beware the Tendency to Negotiate on the Overt Fight Content

Many couples in marital counseling are guided to negotiate on overt subjects of conflict. Oftentimes the contracts that result from these negotiations don't work because the couples never addressed their real conflict—that is, the feelings underlying their overt issue. Since emotions can be so painful, the mind will often cut off from the feelings and focus on behaviors.

For example, instead of admitting to yourself that you feel hurt and frightened when your mate comes home late, you may be inclined to confront him on his various actions. *Why didn't he call? What was he doing? Who was he with?* Once you veer off onto a discussion of behaviors, the natural progression is to negotiate a contract that outlines more acceptable behaviors. It sounds good on paper. But the feelings of fear, hurt, and anger were not addressed. They have gone underground and will reappear in another form at another time. Hence, negotiating won't resolve the true issue—the feelings of insecurity and anger. When negotiation proves ineffective in solving an area of conflict, you must always assume that feelings were brushed under the emotional rug.

Lilly was hurt and angry that her partner never pitched in to help her around the house. For years the couple worked in therapy and negotiated numerous contracts, to no avail. When Lilly came to see me, she bemoaned the fact that her partner didn't care. I quickly realized why contracting had never worked for this couple. Her partner had not understood how she felt about handling it all. Lilly had been the Cinderella of her family of origin and was forced to do all the work while her sister lounged on the couch. Lilly had unconsciously re-created her family of origin, and no amount of contracting was going to take this problem away. She needed to realize first what Old Scar she was trying to heal through her repetitive fights. Then she had to decide to relinquish her old role as Cinderella. Once she reached this level of realization and resolution, she could explain to her partner how his behavior made her feel and resolve this impasse.

I hope you now understand why the emotions that underlie your conflictual issues must be addressed before you can even think about negotiating. But here's where things get a little tricky.

Your Emotional Core

Beneath the feelings that we're aware of lurk even deeper feelings that we may not know. And if you want to resolve your conflicts, you will need to go beyond the overt emotional layer and access what I call your *Emotional Core*—the deepest part of yourself. Unless you unearth your core feelings, you'll have little hope of resolving your conflicts. In order to help you do this, in this following section I detail situations that commonly arise in relationships and help you identify the core feelings that are likely to be aroused in each case.

"Where Were You? Who Were You With?"

When you find yourself interrogating your mate, the overt feelings that accompany your third degree are jealousy or anger. But the obsession that your husband is out with someone else can conceal a core fear of abandonment.

"You Always Take His [or Her] Side Over Mine"

When your partner sides against you—by aligning with one of your children or with his parents, by undermining your rules, or by bribing the kids with money or treats— your overt feeling is anger. But the core feelings are likely to be hurt and a sense of betrayal.

"You Don't Give Me Enough Money"

When you aren't given enough money either because your partner is stingy or because he spends the money on himself and his toys, your overt reaction is probably anger over not being considered. Your pocket may be empty, but your heart is even emptier. And your core feeling is that of being unloved.

"You're Sinking Our Financial Ship"

When your mate spends excessively, empties the savings account, charges the credit cards to the max, or is erratic in paying bills, your overt emotional reactions may be anger and outrage; feelings of powerlessness; or a sense of being out of control, abandoned, and betrayed. The core feeling in this case is fear that you won't survive.

"You Don't Give Me Enough Sex
[or the Right Kind of Sex]"

When you feel deprived in the sex department, the overt reaction is often hurt or anger. A feeling of rejection often lurks beneath, and even deeper may be the feeling that you're starving for love.

"You Don't Let Me In"

When you feel emotionally shut out by your mate, the overt reaction is often anger, loneliness, and hurt. Beneath these feelings may be a core emotion of insecurity or a fear of abandonment.

"Honey, Pass the Beer—and Don't Block the TV"

If your partner doesn't lift a finger around the house, or lounges while you're doing all the chores or child care, you will probably feel used and angry. On the core level, you may feel demeaned and worthless.

"You Don't Spend Enough Time with Me or the Kids"

When your mate places his life, his business, his hobbies, or his friends ahead of you and the children, you may feel hurt and angry on the overt level. On the core emotional level, you'll probably feel rejected and worthless.

"You Don't Tell Me You Love Me"

If you feel deprived of verbal affection, you will probably feel hurt and angry on the overt emotional level. But this issue may conceal an even deeper feeling of worthlessness.

"What Happened to the Wine and Roses?"

If your partner has stopped romancing you, you'll probably feel hurt, neglected, and angry. But at your core, you probably feel unloved, unwanted, and also worthless.

"You're Not My Father"

When your mate controls you, you'll probably be aware of feeling angry and defiant. On the core level, you may actually be feeling inadequate and devalued.

♡

There are many reasons why I encourage you to access the core feelings that lurk beneath your overt emotional reactions. For one thing, when your emotional toes have been stomped on, your initial reaction is usually anger. Even if you don't act on that anger, your partner may still view you as a witch on wheels, and you know what will happen then. By contrast, when you reach inside yourself and access your deeper emotions—the feelings that are beneath the anger—and communicate them to your mate, there will often be an instant shift in him. Faced with your Emotional Core, his own feelings of love, empathy, and caring will be naturally aroused. Then, one of two outcomes usually occurs: either he will alter his behavior spontaneously or he will be more willing to negotiate a modification.

This is why embarking on a negotiation before your mate understands the emotional significance an issue holds for you will lead to a poor outcome. Without this understanding, your request for a behavioral change will make him feel resentful, as if he's being forced to yield just because you want him to. What you want is a willing change, not a forced one.

♡

To sum up this chapter, I have presented three classes of nonnegotiable issues: violations of Relationship Laws, Value Conflicts, and Emotional States.

Violations of Relationship Laws simply need to be stopped, not negotiated.

Value Conflicts are nonnegotiable; however, the behaviors that arise out of these conflicts may or may not be negotiable. And as I have said, the emotions that are stirred as a result of differing values can certainly be handled in the same way that you will address your Emotional States.

If you believe that you're dealing with a negotiable issue, I still suggest that you address the Emotional States surrounding your issue first, following the recommendations in this chapter and the chapter that follows.

The mere act of opening your heart and truthfully sharing the impact of your mate's behavior may be sufficient to stop the upsetting behavior, in which case you'll be able to stop short of a full-scale negotiation. This is often true, but there will be occasions in which your partner will still be resistant to changing his actions. When you're dealing with entrenched behaviors such as bad habits, disagreements over the division of household chores or childcare tasks, the allocation of money, or other similar conflicts, negotiation may be the only answer.

Chapter 10

THE PEACE TREATY:

How to Negotiate a Contract

You are now ready to learn how to negotiate a contract. Years of research have proved to me that how you introduce your subject of conflict is key to a successful outcome. If your issue is not properly introduced, your partner will be gone before you can get past the starting gate, let alone make it to the finish line.

Why Do I Have to Do All the Work?

Many women don't object to initiating conflict discussions, so long as their issues are presented in destructive ways—such as laying blame, complaining, criticizing, and so on—but when they are asked to be positive and constructive, they balk. ("Why do I have to be the one to change? I'm tired of doing all the work. And why do I have to be the one to bring up the problems anyway?") You may feel annoyed, but you have to face facts: women are the relationship watchdogs, meaning that they are the ones to notice problems; they are the relationship overseers and maintainers. So how can a man initiate a discussion around a problem that he doesn't see?

Keep in mind that your resistance to changing how you address your conflict discussions may conceal a fear of relinquishing your armor of anger. You can continue to do what you've been doing or you can do what works. The choice is yours. If you want to achieve resolution, then the next step is to learn to introduce your problems for discussion in a constructive way.

Getting Started

Let's start with your feelings. Something was said or done that you didn't like. Maybe you felt hurt or angry. Get it into your head that the specific feelings and actions that triggered your reaction don't really matter. I'm not saying that your feelings don't count. The point is that from the point of view of conflict-resolution techniques, the issues and feelings are immaterial. The techniques you'll be using to communicate your feelings will remain relatively constant.

Self-Work

Before you bring your problem to your mate, you will need to complete some Self-Work tasks that include:

identifying the Old Scars that the conflict rekindles; recognizing the Fight Traps you feel like using; draining off the emotional venom; digging up love; preparing your Icebreaker (which announces that a problem exists), your Lead-In (which is a supportive statement), and your Problem Statement; determining whether or not you're dealing with a negotiable issue; and preparing for a full-scale negotiation, if this applies.

After reading the list above, you may feel tempted to simply bash your mate over the head and skip the Self-Work. I understand the temptation, but where will giving up get you? Either in jail or out of the relationship! So, for your own sake, don't give up now. Riding a bike seemed daunting at first, as do the Self-Work tasks. But once you become familiar with them and practice a bit, the tasks will no longer seem overwhelming. So let's look at these tasks more closely.

Identify the Old Scar

Figuring out what Old Scar has been activated by your mate's words or actions will help you redirect your focus away from your partner and onto the ghosts of the past.

It would be good to figure out what Old Scars your current fight may have stirred in your mate as well. This information will assist you in creating a Problem Statement that is most suited to your mate's needs. What's more, the better you understand what is happening emotionally for your mate, the more you'll be able to keep the discussions on track or steer him or her back on track when the discussion derails.

Recognize Your Fight Traps

During this next portion of Self-Work, note whatever fears you have about bringing your issue to your mate. Do you fear that your mate will be unreceptive to you? Do you think that your directness will make matters worse? Based upon past disasters, your fear is probably well founded.

Your fear may also be warning you that your creature-of-habit brain is threatening to rear its ugly head. That is, your unconscious mind may try to trick you into saying or doing things to get your mate riled up so that he (as well as you) will act in the old, familiar ways. So don't write off these fears so fast; they're telling you something very important. And if you're afraid of a bad outcome, be extra careful to recognize and not to play out your old Fight Traps. Remember, falling into Fight Traps may float your boat in the moment, but your relationship will sink in the end.

Drain Off Raw Rage

Lisette was terrified to speak to her husband about her issue for fear that he would bite her head off. Soon, Lisette discovered that she was actually afraid of her own anger—she actually wanted to destroy her husband, Scott, verbally. Holding back was a defense against her secret wish to let herself rip. In order to move past this sticking point, Lisette needed to admit how angry she was with her husband and drain off the emotional venom.

Like Lisette, you, too, will need to drain off your rage so that you are as cool as possible when bringing your issue to your mate. A good way to do this is to fantasize exactly how you would do your mate in. Do you want to brain him with a frying pan? Or Krazy Glue his lips shut and beat him senseless with a rubber bat? Whatever fantasy you choose is harmless so long as you know that you can't and won't act on it. So, fantasize away and mentally drain off all your anger. When you're finished, you will feel emptied out and almost ready to approach your mate with a cool head. But draining off your rage isn't all that's needed. You also need to access your feelings of love.

Dig Up Love

It's difficult to access feelings of love when you're feeling angry with your mate. This is because when you're upset, your mind tends to associate the currently upsetting event with memories of similar instances in which your mate let you down. When this happens, your mind "floods" with bad memories and you find yourself drowning in negative feelings. The only way around this impasse is to consciously choose to stop the flow of negative associations by reminding yourself that the present need not be automatically connected to the past. Once you've stopped yourself from flooding, you need to go one step further and remind yourself that you're overlooking the good aspects of your relationship and your mate. And once this is done, you're ready to dig up love by recalling memories of special moments with your partner and/or reminding yourself of the qualities you love about him or her.

After completing these four tasks, you'll be emotionally ready to move on to the next phase of Self-Work: preparing the wording for your Icebreaker, Lead-In, and Problem

Statement. The goal is to choose words and phrases that you know will open your mate's ears and heart. Let's start with the Icebreaker.

Prepare the Icebreaker

An Icebreaker is a sentence that alerts your mate that you need to discuss a problem. I suggest that your Icebreaker be as neutral as possible. You don't want to be seen as a you-know-what breaker. Ill-worded Icebreakers such as "We have to talk right now" or "You've done it again" are sure to get your mate's back up; you can forget the dream of seeing a healthy discussion unfold if his fur is bristling. More preferable are sentences like "I have something that's bothering me. Is this a good time for us to talk?" or "I need your help with something. Do you have some time to talk with me now?" When you deliver the Icebreaker, make sure that you adopt neutral body language and speak in a cool vocal tone.

Prepare the Lead-In

Next, prepare the wording for the Lead-In. This is a positive statement that puts your mate at ease, guards against ANS arousal, and creates a loving and safe climate for your discussion or negotiation. In the Lead-In, you will state why your mate is important to you, what you value about your relationship, or what traits you admire in him or her. Keying into traits that will facilitate the upcoming negotiation kills two relationship birds with one stone.

The Lead-In may also include knowledge of self or other. Here you may allude to Old Scars, if you think it would be helpful. Mentioning your mate's Old Scars can convey that you understand why the particular problem you're about to discuss will be painful or difficult to face. For example, you might say, "I know that you were criticized as a kid and that confrontations can be painful for you." By conveying your knowledge of your mate's Old Scars, you're positioning yourself as a friend who wishes to do no harm. Be careful not to wield his Old Scars like a baseball bat, bashing, mocking, or belittling him. For example, statements like "You never grew up" or "You're just like your father" are attacks and do not set the stage for a constructive discussion.

Sample Lead-Ins

"I value our relationship and the love we share . . ."
"You are very special to me . . ."
"I have always admired your willingness to face problems head-on."

When the Lead-In is prepared, move on to creating your Problem Statement.

Prepare the Problem Statement: Basic Considerations

The Positive Confrontation

No matter how you sweeten the blow, delivering a Problem Statement is a confrontation. Most distressed couples have mastered the art of negative confrontation, which consists of emotional purging or "getting it off your chest." But as you know, letting yourself emotionally rip never succeeds and always harms the relationship. So remember, this is not the time for emotional venting. You should have already drained off the intensity of your feelings during Self-Work, and if you haven't, you shouldn't be addressing your conflict yet.

In fact, you should not approach your mate for discussion until you're ready to provide a positive confrontation that will set the proper climate and make your mate feel worthwhile, at ease, and motivated to want to move deeper into the negotiation process. It's how you present the confrontation that will set the proper climate and determine if your negotiations move forward or not.

Don't Express

As I've told you throughout this book, your chances of resolution will depend upon your ability to stay cool, and this is especially true when you introduce your Problem Statement. Your goal is to *present* what upset you and to *describe,* not *express,* your emotional reaction. The cooler and more detached you are, the greater your chances for a successful discussion.

One Issue at a Time

When presenting your issue, focus on one problem and only one. Don't forget that many women find it natural to bring up every bothersome issue (the Kitchen Sink Fight Trap) instead of focusing on the one issue at hand. If you throw in everything that has upset you since day one, your mate's ANS arousal will kick into high gear, and you know what will happen. So, even if you have several issues to address, remember that Rome wasn't built in a day. We'll get to them all eventually. The key is to not overwhelm your mate by presenting more than one issue. As I often tell women, "Don't bite off more than he can chew."

Don't Respond in the Moment

As a final note, I do not advise you to respond in the moment that you are offended. You risk opening the discussion in a way that is less than ideal. What's more, when you tell your mate what's troubling you, you must be prepared to move directly into a conflict discussion and possible negotiation. And if you haven't taken the time to perform all the Self-Work steps, you won't be ready. So until you're very proficient at resolving your conflicts, I recommend that you wait to talk to your partner until you've completed all of your Self-Work. Now, let's move on to constructing your Problem Statement.

Creating Your Problem Statement

There is a scientifically recognized formula for properly presenting your issue for discussion. The formula is in three parts: (1) the Disclaimer, (2) the Presentation of Your Issue, and (3) the Suggestion for the Future. Let's begin with the Disclaimer.

The Disclaimer

Presenting your problem to a mate whose ego is fragile or eroded (which is the case for most people in a distressed relationship) is a losing proposition. Your partner will feel wounded by the most innocent remarks, and will resort to making excuses, defending, denying, and counterblaming in an unconscious attempt to pad his psyche. You can't put your problem to someone who must ward off everything you say in order to stay mentally afloat.

Here's where the Disclaimer comes in. It assures your mate that you're on his side, even during a confrontation. It protects his psyche so that he no longer needs to bandage himself with excuses, defensiveness, and denial. When your mate's ego is insulated, he'll be more willing to listen to your issue.

Sample Disclaimers

"I know you didn't mean to hurt [or upset] me."
"I'm sure you didn't realize how you were coming across."
"I know you love me [and the kids] and you don't want to hurt my (our) feelings."

As you can see, the Disclaimer gives your mate the benefit of the doubt. When he feels that you aren't blaming him, he'll no longer need to defend himself. If you're still thinking, *My partner knows very well what he's doing to upset me, and giving him the benefit of the doubt would be a flat-out lie* or *I've told him a thousand times what bothers me*, remember, you can't say with 100 percent assurance that he ever heard what you said. Until recently, chronic ANS arousal made him deaf to your words.

If you're still skeptical, you have my permission to retain your doubts. In fact, believe, if you like, that the Disclaimer will make no difference. Just use it anyway and watch centuries' worth of wax dissolve from his ears.

After you've presented your Disclaimer, your mate will be primed and ready for you to present your issue.

Presentation of Your Issue: The X, Y Formula

The proper way to present your issue is using the *X, Y* Formula, which consists of describing your mate's upsetting behavior and then stating how you feel: "When you do *x*, I feel *y*."

Notice that I told you to focus on the *behavior* that upset you. By focusing on your mate's behavior, rather than on his person, you'll be protecting his ego, which will keep his ANS arousal on ice.

It's also possible to reverse the order of the *X, Y* Formula and say, "I felt *y* when you said or did *x*." Based upon what you know about your mate, you'll need to decide whether he would respond better if you were to lead with a description of your feelings instead of a description of his upsetting behavior.

Keep in mind that when you say "I feel," a highly defensive partner may be inclined to throw your words back in your face: "So, that's what you feel. That's your problem, not mine!" The translation of this statement is "Don't blame me; my ego is too fragile to tolerate being wrong." If your mate exhibits such defensiveness, you can be sure that his ego needs to be handled with kid gloves. And don't be fooled—even if he's a physical Mighty Man, he may actually be an emotional Minnie Mouse. The challenge then becomes how to prevent a fragile partner from blowing an emotional gasket. There is hope. In addition to the de-escalating effect of the Disclaimer, there is another technique that will help your mate swallow your Problem Statement.

Avoid the Word *You*

When a fragile person hears "*You* did *x, y,* or *z,*" he feels that a finger is being pointed at his ego, and you know what that means. You can take his ego off the hook by rewording your *X, Y* Formula so that the word *you* isn't said at all. For example, "I feel *x* . . . when *y* happens" or "I feel *x* . . . when *y* is said (or done) to me."

Prepare the Suggestion for the Future

Your Problem Statement will be complete when you add the Suggestion for the Future. Remember, men feel at a loss to translate your distress into concrete solutions. Without your suggestion on how he can improve or please you in the future, he'll feel like he's drowning in a sea of complaints. Your Suggestion for the Future appeals to the concrete, goal-oriented side of a man that says, "Tell me what to do and I'll do it."

Devising a clear Suggestion for the Future is a hard skill for many women to acquire because, as I've said before, it's much easier for us to say what our partners are doing wrong than it is to formulate a clear, concise statement of the behavior we would prefer from our mates.

The inability often stems from a deep-seated resistance to state what we need. This wish is often expressed in sentences like "If I have to tell my husband what I need, it isn't worth it" or "If he loved me, he'd know what I need." As I said in Chapter 8, this wish stems from insufficient or absent mothering early in life. You must remind yourself that no partner can make up for such early deficits. So remember, if you want to stay unhappy, keep hoping that he'll guess your every need. And while you're at it, hope that he'll sprout breasts, too. You have an equal chance of both things happening.

Another reason why you may find it hard to construct a concise Suggestion for the Future is that, as you know, women haven't been socialized to speak in concrete, goal-oriented terms. This explains why you will probably find it easier to say, "Be nice to me" (vague and general) instead of "I'd feel special if you asked me out to dinner on Friday night." Or you might say, "You don't pay any attention to me anymore" (vague, general, critical, complaining) instead of "I'd like you to sit next to me and listen while I talk to you." In order for your Problem Statement to be effective, you'll need to speak more like a male and directly state the behavioral change that you're seeking.

Put the Steps Together

When all of these steps are put together, the way you present your problem to your mate will play something like the following scenario.

The Icebreaker

"Honey, do you have some time to talk with me?"
(You are told yes.)

The Lead-In

"I know how hard you've been trying to work with me on resolving our conflicts, and I appreciate your efforts."

The Disclaimer

"I'm sure you didn't realize that I would be upset, but . . ."

Presentation of Your Issue: The *X, Y* Formula

"When x is done to me [avoid the word you], I feel y."
Or, you may reverse the order and state the feeling first and the behavioral description second.
"I feel x when y is said [or done] to me." (Avoid the word you.)

The Suggestion for the Future

"But in the future, I would feel so happy if you would do or say x."

Planning your words may sound contrived to you. It is. And I want you to engage in and practice this cumbersome process because it guards against the tendency to blurt out words before considering their effect. We don't want to turn your mate off before discussions have begun.

Before delivering any of these statements, however, you still have one final Self-Work task: to determine whether or not you are dealing with a negotiable issue. Remember, Emotional States, Value Conflicts, and violations of Relationship Laws are nonnegotiable. Refer to the previous chapter to refresh your memory on the distinction between negotiable and nonnegotiable issues.

♡

Now that you've completed the Self-Work tasks, you are ready to begin your conflict discussion, starting with the delivery of the Icebreaker. But before you break the ice, make sure that your mate is available.

Knock Before Entering

If you knock on your mate's psychological door, rather than barging in, your mate will be more responsive to you. An excellent way to knock is to ask, "Do you have some time for me?" or "Are you busy right now?" If your mate says you may proceed, then deliver your Icebreaker right away.

After you've delivered a prize-winning Icebreaker, a couple of things may happen. You may notice reluctance on your mate's part (more like dread) to agree to talk further with you. Remember, previous discussions made him want to run for cover, so realize that if he isn't jumping for joy, it's only past experience talking. If he seems less than eager to talk, you might say, "Listen, I don't want to rip your head off. I just need your input on a problem."

When you deliver your Icebreaker, you need to be prepared for the possibility that your mate may not offer you the green light to pursue the matter at this time, in which case you'll need to schedule a discussion for later—ideally during the same day.

You will also be facing a postponement if your mate becomes too defensive to continue. That will require you to reconsider your approach, and try it again at a later time.

If, for whatever reason, your talk has been postponed, you both need to schedule an exact time, date, and place (excluding the bedroom or wherever else you have sex).

If your mate says that he would like to talk later, he still may want a clue regarding what you'll be discussing down the line. Knowing your mate as you do, you must decide if it's better to give him a hint of what is troubling you, even though you won't be actually discussing the matter until later.

For some men, knowing the nature of the problem in advance of the actual discussion works well. It can provide a feeling of being in control, enable them to digest the initial shock, diminish the fear of the unknown, and even offer an interval of time in which they can begin working on the problem. After all, most men do like to solve their problems independently.

On a related note, not knowing what will be discussed later can make your partner feel like a kid being called to the principal's office to be reamed out for some unknown offense. If your mate was often in the doghouse as a child, not telling him what the problem is about and making him wait until later may transform you, in his unconscious mind, into an authority figure. If these associations occur, ANS arousal will be cranked up, and you can kiss your talk goodbye. For such men, alluding to your issue in advance of the actual discussion can be helpful.

For other spouses, knowing your issue ahead of time can backfire in a big way. Clueing him in on what you'll be discussing later may trigger a defensive reaction that you're not prepared to work through in the moment.

Another danger of giving too much information in advance is that he may become anxious that a confrontation will erupt down the road (especially if your first approach made him hot under the collar), his ANS arousal will mount, and he may be in withdrawal before you get to the bargaining table.

So you need to decide whether it would be best to leave the problem vague until the scheduled talk time. If you decide that this is best, merely deflect questions like "What's it all about?" by saying, "Honey, I don't want to rush us. I'll look forward to your input later, when we'll have more time." Make sure that you keep the atmosphere light and nonthreatening when you say that; otherwise, your mate will become anxious between now and when you actually sit down to talk. In which case, there will be no talk.

If your mate takes the bait and agrees to talk immediately, then you'll deliver your Lead-In and Problem Statement. I remind you again that the Problem Statement opens the door to your conflict discussion and possible negotiations, so you must be sure that all your Self-Work is complete before you deliver your Problem Statement.

You'll also need to master the next section before you deliver your Problem Statement. Otherwise your discussion will be cut off at the knees.

Switching Battle Gear:
Becoming the Discussion Overseer

After you deliver your Problem Statement, be prepared to make an immediate, 180-degree shift in roles from confronter to discussion overseer. Keep in mind that even if you deliver a perfect Problem Statement, your discussion may still jump the tracks. Your job as overseer is to keep a finger on your mate's emotional pulse, watch for signs of ANS arousal, and make sure that your discussion doesn't derail.

Remember to listen to and watch the verbal and nonverbal aspects of your partner's behavior. Is he beginning to justify himself (verbal cue)? Is he avoiding eye contact (nonverbal cue)? The following is a quick checklist to refresh your memory on the signs of mounting ANS arousal.

Nonverbal Cues

- His voice starts to rise.

- He seems overheated (sweating), and is red in the face or breathing heavily.

- He is exhibiting early signs of withdrawal behavior: gives a blank, emotionless stare; turns away; avoids eye contact; or appears to be not hearing, is silent, or looks sullen.

- He looks ready to bolt from the room.

Verbal Cues

- He has started to justify or defend himself, refuses to accept responsibility, or makes excuses.
- He is counterblaming.
- He has begun repeating himself.

First Aid

If you observe any of the above signs of ANS arousal, you must employ what I call First Aid immediately or else the discussion is going to tank. The goal of your repair efforts is to smooth your mate's ruffled feathers using my various First Aid techniques, which are conflict de-escalation or Cool-Down tactics.

Time to Bring Up Ancient History

One way to smooth your mate's ruffling feathers is to Bring Up Ancient History. I don't mean that you should dredge up past grievances with your partner; that would only inflame matters more. I mean that it may be helpful to tell your mate what Old Scars have been triggered by your current conflict. This technique is effective for two reasons: (1) it immediately sparks empathy on the part of your mate because he can see the hurting child in you, and (2) talking about pain that stems from before he was in the picture shifts the focus away from his ego, which aborts ANS arousal and withdrawal reactions.

"When you tell me that we can't ever go out to dinner, no discussion, it reminds me of my father, who never let me tell him my point of view. It made me feel so hurt and frustrated when Dad did that to me."

Admit to the More Vulnerable Feelings That Underlie Anger

Another way to cool down the climate is to focus on the vulnerable feelings that we often conceal with anger. For example, if your mate comes home late for dinner and hasn't bothered to call, rather than blasting him with anger, it's far more effective to admit that you felt scared that something happened to him. When you speak from a more vulnerable place, this should help your mate be more receptive and less defensive.

Cool-Down Questions to Refocus a Mate Who's Losing It

Presuming that your mate's ANS arousal isn't off the charts, the following Cool-Down questions can also be effective in settling your partner down.

"Obviously I'm not coming across properly. Can you help me rephrase what I'm saying in a way that would feel better for you?"

"I think that you're feeling attacked by me. That is not my intent. Can you tell me where I'm going wrong?"

"Can you suggest how I could talk to you in a way that won't offend you?"

There are also First Aid techniques designed to handle the following specific meltdowns. The goal in all cases remains the same—to shore up an ego that is fraying in order to arrest ANS arousal.

He Makes Excuses, Defends His Behavior, or Justifies Himself

When your mate begins to tell you all the reasons why he did what he did, he is obviously feeling blamed or attacked. His ego needs patching or else he'll be out the door any second.

Response: "I'm not saying you intentionally set out to hurt [or whatever the feeling is] me. I'm just telling you how I feel" or "I'm just telling you how the behavior landed with me."

He Says, "But What About My Feelings?"

In a perfect world, you, the confronter, should be heard and completely understood before your mate takes his turn to state his own thoughts and feelings. I call this the Emotional Right-of-Way. Distressed partners are so accustomed to not being heard that they have a hard time waiting their turn. This explains why your boyfriend or husband will demand his own airtime before you have finished speaking. ("You feel sad or mad . . . How do you think I feel?" or "You want me to listen to your feelings, but what about mine?")

When you feel cut off, your natural reaction will be to interrupt him, which will further contribute to his feeling of not being heard. While you, the confronter, have the

Emotional Right-of-Way, you need to keep your eye on the larger goal: saving the negotiation.

You have two ways to proceed at this point. One is to tell your mate: "I am interested in how you feel. Can we finish with me and then get back to you?" The acknowledgment that you're interested in his feelings often helps to bring the discussion back on track. But if it doesn't, you have only one other choice: deal with his feelings, let him talk, use your learned listening skills, and reflect your understanding of his feelings. When he feels emotionally understood, you should be able to resume the original discussion and get back to you.

Interrupting

This discussion impasse is similar to the one discussed above. When your partner interrupts you, for whatever reason, you need to know that he's feeling attacked and is on the defensive. Warning bells should go off for you: ANS arousal is mounting. You need to cool things down, and fast.

Response: "You have a good point there. Can we agree to get back to it after we finish this?" or "I think you're feeling blamed by me . . . how can I talk to you so you won't feel so upset?" or "Are you interrupting because you aren't feeling heard by me?"

You Shouldn't Feel That Way

As I've said elsewhere, since men feel responsible for their partners' happiness, they also think that it's their job to rescue them when they're upset. This causes your mate to try to talk you out of your feelings. ("Let it go" or "It's not a big deal" or "You're being too sensitive.") A good response is "I know you don't like the feelings in the air. If you listen and understand, my feelings will settle down more quickly."

If you sense that your mate is trying to talk you out of your feelings because he feels guilty for having inflicted pain on you, the following response is ideal: "I think you're feeling guilty, and I want you to know that I understand that you didn't mean to hurt me. Just understanding me now will help me feel better."

Counterblaming

Your mate is trying to shore up his ego by saying, "I'm not the bad guy; you make mistakes, too."

Response: "You have a valid point about me. Could we finish what we're talking about now and get back to what I've done to upset you after we finish this?"

Refusal to Accept Responsibility

When a man's ego is eroded, accepting responsibility for upsetting you is tantamount to admitting that he is a failure.

Response: "I know that you didn't mean to hurt [or whatever the feeling is] me when you did x, y, or z. Making a mistake doesn't mean you're bad. We're just talking about this particular instance." Or you might say, "If you accidentally fell on my foot and broke it, I'd still be in pain. I need you to understand that my feelings were accidentally hurt, too."

Another possible block to accepting responsibility stems from the fear of vulnerability. Your mate may be afraid that his admission of "guilt" will be used against him. If you suspect that this is the case, then the following would apply: "Listen, just because you acknowledge that you did something to hurt me doesn't mean that I'm going to get even or never let you live it down."

Summarizing Self

It has been observed that distressed couples summarize and restate their positions during conflict discussions. When spouses are not feeling heard by each other, they repeat themselves hoping to be finally heard. If you notice that your mate is beginning to repeat himself, it's time to get into high listening gear. And you'd better act fast, because not feeling heard is ANS arousal bait. You might say something like "I notice you've repeated that sentence a couple of times. Did you think that I didn't hear you?" or "Obviously I haven't given you the impression that I have heard and understood what you're saying. Let me repeat what I think you're saying, and you tell me if I've understood."

If All Else Fails, Abort Mission

If your mate's ANS arousal is off the charts, you may not be able to veer your discussion back on track. If you cannot succeed in cooling things down despite the First Aid techniques described in the previous section, then abort your discussion and postpone it until later. Use this interval to analyze where the discussion went wrong. Ask your mate for feedback on what he thinks caused the discussion to derail, using the Cool-Down questions mentioned above. And use your accumulated knowledge to refine your approach.

♡

Let's assume that your discussion has progressed smoothly, except for one problem. Your request for change has not been received with open arms, and you're miles away from a resolution of your issue. Where do you go from here?

Time to Negotiate

We are finally ready to discuss those situations in which negotiating a contract is in order. If I asked you to define the goal of negotiation, I bet you'd say something like "to compromise" or "to meet each other halfway." You're not alone in assuming that negotiation is synonymous with compromise. In fact, most marriage counselors, pastors, and mediators advise distressed couples to "cut the apple in half"—but who in his or her right mind wants half the apple? Compromise, by its very nature, leaves both parties unsatisfied and, for this reason, rarely produces the desired results. This probably explains why most couples approach the negotiation process with the enthusiasm reserved for a root canal. Well, unclench your teeth. I'm not asking you to compromise. What we're after is collaboration.

Collaboration, by contrast with compromise, is an active process in which both partners put their heads to-gether and devise a creative and unique resolution to their conflict. Even though it takes a bit more effort, you'll find that this method produces better negotiation outcomes and greater relationship satisfaction. For these reasons, it's well worth the extra effort.

How to Create a Winning Contract

There are a number of elements that make up a good marital contract.

Be a Friend

In order to negotiate a contract that works, you must be willing to trash your guns and ammunition and address your mate from the perspective of a caring friend.

Be Clear and Specific

To create a winning contract, you'll need to clarify the specific details, including dates, times, places, frequencies, and anything else you can think of. In addition, you'll need to make sure that you clearly define the behavioral changes that are outlined in the contract. For example, "I promise to be nice to you" is vague and general. Instead, your contract needs to target specific, observable behaviors. A better statement would be "I promise to take ten minutes each evening to give you my undivided attention."

Outline Positive Changes

If your expected behavioral changes are formulated in a positive, not negative, way, you're both more likely to be satisfied with your contract. Stating what you expect from each other enables you to focus your energies on meeting each other's needs. However, if your contract is framed in the negative sense ("I won't do *x*"), all your attention will be placed on not throwing grenades at each other. While you may reach a cease-fire, you won't be meeting each other's needs or resolving your issues.

Manageable Contracts

How many times have you noticed the failure of New Year's resolutions? "I will lose 8 million pounds by tomorrow and I will jog 10,000 miles twice a day." You know how people set themselves up with unreasonable goals, only to fail. So make sure that the behavioral changes outlined in your contract are small and manageable. You can always expand on the contract in a later negotiation.

The Contract Isn't Carved in Stone

If your contracts are viewed as irrevocable, they will be doomed to failure. For one thing, one or both of you may be reluctant to close the deal for fear that there will be no turning back—especially if the contract doesn't work. A contract should never feel like a life sentence without parole. Don't worry that you're offering your partner a bailout clause. Remember, his previous broken commitments were due to flawed negotiations or chronic ANS arousal, rather than bad intentions.

I Won't Squash You

If your mate was squashed during his formative years, he will unconsciously equate negotiating with "giving in" or "being defeated," which will lead to extremely defensive, uncooperative behavior. Your mate needs to know that you don't intend to shove your agenda down his throat. In giving this message, you become a source of safety, rather than danger. In this atmosphere, you both can feel safe to negotiate.

Seek Input

The best way to convey that you won't squash your mate is to seek his input on possible solutions. Doing so puts him in the driver's seat and sets you up as a friend rather than a controlling parent. You must also beware of a potential setup. If your mate's parent(s) always told him what to do, he may induce you to provide all the suggested solutions. And if you do so, he may view you as his bossy parent, in which case there is a great danger that he'll sabotage the contract. So remember to ask your mate for suggestions on how to resolve your issue. Once all the options are on the table, discuss each one fully. Explore how you both will feel if this versus that option is selected. The key here is that you're seeking your mate's input, not shoving orders down an enemy's throat.

Mutuality

In order for your contract to be a success, you must remember one key word: *mutuality.* If the negotiations are lopsided in favor of a one-sided contract, the contract will fail. One-sided contracts leave the person who must do the changing feeling like a scolded child whose parent is forcing him to behave. Resentment and contract sabotage will follow. Not only must you both contribute equally to the creation of the contract, but the contract must also outline changes that will be made by both of you.

Put the Deal in Writing

So there is no room for confusion, it's best to commit your contracts to paper and post them conspicuously. By writing down your contracts, you lend a businesslike feel to the relationship. Some couples like this and others don't. The obvious advantage of a written contract is that it's harder to weasel out of it. On the other hand, if your mate felt controlled as a kid, feeling obliged to write down a contract may give him a backed-into-the-corner feeling, which could result in sabotage. So, rather than force your mate to write down the contract, discuss its pros and cons. Because the agreement is mutual, and behavioral changes are promised on both sides, your mate shouldn't feel too reluctant to commit it to paper. Remember, the written contract is for both of you, not just for him.

How Will We Know That the Contract Is a Success?

Within the body of the contract, you both need to spell out the criteria you will use to evaluate the contract. Will feelings be the guide—that is, "The contract feels good to me; how about you?" Will you judge the contract based upon ease of use? It's up to you both to decide. If you've chosen to write down your contract, you'll include the criteria for success or failure in the body of the document.

When Will We Meet to Renegotiate?

The final feature of the contract is the provision for renegotiation. You both must agree on the date, time, and place at which you will get together to discuss whether or not the contract was a success. If one or both of you decide that the contract requires renegotiation, you will do so at the follow-up meeting. If you've decided to write down your contract, the follow-up date will be included. At the follow-up meeting, be prepared to conduct a new negotiation using the same steps described above.

The Quid Pro Quo Contract

Now that you're clear on the basic requirements of a good agreement, let's discuss the most popular form of intimate relationship contract: the Quid Pro Quo Contract. This produces the best outcomes due to its inherent mutuality. Both partners agree to make behavioral changes. For example: "I promise to remind you once and only once to help Johnny with his homework. In return for my not nagging you, you agree to help Johnny for a half hour each night."

The benefit of this form of contracting—its mutuality—can also be its demise; since both partners are expected to alter their behavior, scorekeeping can result ("I did my part of the bargain three times and you held up your end only once"). If you or your partner is inclined to keep score, be very careful. In your case, it would be much better to frame the contract in terms of "I'm making this change because I love you and want to keep the relationship."

Here is an example of a good contract: "For the next three weeks, I agree to wash the dishes on Monday, Wednesday, and Friday nights so that you can do your schoolwork. You agree to babysit the kids on Tuesday and Thursday evenings from seven to nine, and on Saturday mornings from eight to ten, so that I can attend my aerobics class. We agree to meet again on November 9 at noon to evaluate the success of this contract."

Handling a Common Negotiation Impasse: Endless Counterproposals

When negotiating, it's common for couples to become trapped in a net of counterproposals (the "I propose *x*, then you propose *y*" syndrome). When this occurs, you will find it impossible to close the deal. Endless counterproposals can arise when essential elements are missing from your contract. For example, if the solution is one-sided, as opposed to mutual, the overridden spouse may resist concluding the negotiation because the proposed plan doesn't take his ideas into consideration.

Endless counterproposals can also conceal unspoken feelings. For example, a resistance to close the deal may conceal a fear of change or a fear that rocking the boat will only make the relationship worse. These fears may hide an even deeper fear of being disappointed: *If we arrive at a contract and my partner doesn't follow through, I'll be hurt.*

Whenever counterproposals occur, it's good to explore your partner's thoughts and feelings regarding the meaning of the impasse. It is also imperative that both of you use your listening skills to thoroughly understand the feelings and objections to the various proposals on the table. Listening to each other's feelings is often sufficient to move the discussions forward.

Some Negotiation Examples

I'm going to give you a few examples of how various couples negotiated a resolution of their conflicts. In each example, I concentrate on one specific negotiation impasse, and show how the couple moved beyond it.

Example 1

Negotiation Impasse: poorly constructed problem statement leads to an aborted discussion.

Esther was annoyed that her husband, Pierre, always rushed sex. She told him many times, "I've seen animals wait longer!" No matter what Esther said or did, she was unsuccessful in getting through to her husband. She decided to try again, using my method.

She performed Self-Work and paid particular attention to identifying Old Scars. She realized that her husband's refusal to spend more time with her made her feel unloved, the way she did as a child. Regarding Pierre, she recalled that he never felt that he lived up to his parents' expectations. She now realized why he had been so touchy whenever she tried to bring up their sexual problem.

Esther completed the remaining Self-Work tasks and then asked to talk.

She delivered her Icebreaker: "Do you have a minute?" He was calculating the taxes and reluctantly looked up at her. (She had forgotten to Knock Before Entering and had approached him when he was busy. First mistake.)

Next, she gave her Lead-In: "I know you hate to talk about what I'm going to say." (This is a statement of understanding, but not a positive, supportive statement.)

Then she said her Disclaimer: "And I guess you don't mean to upset me, but . . ." (The words *I guess* sounded like she wasn't sure, which landed like an attack—"maybe you *do* mean to upset me.")

Next came the Presentation of the Issue (*X, Y* Formula): "But when you rush sex, I feel unloved." (She used the word *you*, which heightened his feeling of being attacked.)

Then she added her Suggestion for the Future: "I want you to stop going so fast." (The suggestion was presented in a negative fashion, and it indirectly attacked him for going too fast.)

Pierre jumped up and stormed from the room.

Oops. I guess I blew it, Esther said to herself.

She followed him and applied First Aid by saying, "I think I put you on the defensive. Can you tell me where I went wrong?"

He informed her and she told him that she would rethink her approach. They agreed to talk later that day.

When she refined her approach, here's what she did:

She made sure to Knock Before Entering by saying: "Honey, are you busy now? (He gave her the go-ahead.)

She skipped the Icebreaker (he already knew that there was a problem).

Next, she stated her new and improved Lead-In: "I know how you felt put down by your parents, and that's the last thing I want you to feel with me." (She mentions his Old Scar and positions herself as his friend and ally.)

Then she delivered her Disclaimer: "I know you don't realize the effect it has on me . . . but," which she followed by the Presentation of the Issue (the *X, Y* Formula), "when sex is over quickly, I feel unwanted." (She omitted the word *you* and used very neutral phrasing.)

Then she added her Suggestion for the Future: "I want so much to spend more time being close and would value your suggestions on how we can work this out." (The suggestion is presented in a positive fashion and leaves room for his input.)

Esther's new approach helped Pierre stay with the discussion and see it through to resolution.

Example 2

Negotiation Impasse: husband becomes defensive after problem statement is delivered.

Marian and Ed are standing in the bedroom embroiled in a boxer-shorts battle. Each morning, Ed drops his underwear beside the bed, where it remains for days. History has shown that the underwear heap will become taller than Mount Rushmore if Marian doesn't break down and pick up after him.

Marian began by performing her Self-Work tasks. She focused first on understanding both of their Old Scars, and soon realized that she was so angry with her husband because she had been treated like a maid in her first family.

She also keyed in to the fact that Ed's mother bossed and controlled him. So as she prepared the words to kick off her discussion, she made a special effort to ensure that he would not feel squashed by her.

Her Icebreaker, Lead-In, Disclaimer, and Problem Statement were as follows:

- Icebreaker: *"Honey, I need your advice on a problem. Do you have some time to talk to me now?"*

- Lead-In: *"You know how much I appreciate your problem-solving skills, and we need to take advantage of them now."*

- Disclaimer: *"I'm sure you don't mean to upset me, but . . ."*

- Presentation of the Issue (*X, Y* Formula): *"When I have to pick up clothing from the floor, I feel so upset, the same way I felt when my family expected me to be the maid."*

- Suggestion for the Future: *"I would like us to avoid this conflict in the future, and need your ideas on how we can do this."* (Keeping in mind that Ed becomes defensive when he feels told what to do, she presented her suggestion in an open-ended way, leaving room for his input.)

After she finished, Ed said, "Are you telling me that I'm a slob?" (defensive response)

She quickly applied First Aid. "Honey, you're not a slob. I'm just telling you how the laundry pile lands with me."

"You leave your stuff all over the house." (counter-blaming).

"You have a good point, and maybe we should talk about that later." (First Aid)

After a few rounds of Cool-Down techniques, he settled down.

Next, they began the negotiation process. Marian invited Ed to come up with ideas first. Initially he told her that late at night he was too tired to walk to the hamper in the laundry room. She listened to his feelings and told him that she understood. Feeling heard, he came up with a suggestion: that they move the hamper to the master bath—so that he could toss his clothes in it each night without feeling too put out. This solution was satisfactory to both partners. They committed the deal to paper and set a follow-up date to assess the contract.

Example 3

Negotiation Impasse: husband's refusal to entertain his wife's suggestions, and his many counterproposals.

Connie rushed home, her arms loaded with a bag of Chinese food and a video. Doug promised to be home by seven. As usual, he was late. By eight o'clock, the dinner was stone-cold and she was boiling mad.

When Connie did her Self-Work, she discovered that feelings of hurt and terror were lurking beneath her anger. Her father, who was an alcoholic, often wouldn't return home for days, and many times she was frightened that he would never come home again. This explained why she was so upset when Doug came home late. Regarding

Doug, Connie knew that his mother criticized him, and she realized that she needed to be very careful not to arouse his Old Scar.

After she completed all the Self-Work steps, she "knocked" and delivered her Icebreaker: "Doug, do you have some time to help me with a problem?"

When he agreed to talk right away, she stated her Lead-In: "I know how hard you work to support us."

Her Disclaimer: "And I know you don't realize the effect it has on me, but . . ."

Her Presentation of the Issue (the *X, Y* Formula): "When I'm left wondering when you'll come home, I'm filled with terror, like when my dad stayed away."

Her Suggestion for the Future: "And I would feel so loved and safe if I knew when you'd be home for dinner."

Doug was initially silent, but he didn't become defensive. "I see what you mean," he finally said. Since he had received her issue, Connie asked whether he was ready to negotiate. He agreed.

She suggested that they set a later dinnertime, so that he would be sure to make it. Her proposal was met with refusal—"I can't say for sure when I'll be home"—and then with counterproposals that were not in tune with her request: "Instead of holding up dinner, why not eat without me?" She made five other suggestions and they all met with the same fate.

Connie suspected that his refusal and counterproposals were signs that ANS arousal was mounting. She decided to try a Cool-Down question: "I notice that you keep rejecting my ideas. Do you know why?"

He said that her solutions seemed simplistic to him, and it felt like she was telling him that he was too dumb to think for himself. She listened, understood, and reflected her understanding back to him.

Having felt understood, he then came up with a suggestion. "The reason why I can't tell you when I'll be home is because the traffic on my route is unpredictable, and you know how I feel about using my cell phone while I'm driving. But if I get comfortable using the hands-free settings, I'll be able to keep in touch with you all the time."

There was no need to commit their agreement to paper or meet to renegotiate. The issue was resolved.

♡

Having read the preceding examples, you may feel that the negotiation process is too involved or too difficult to put into practice. Have no fear. Each time you negotiate, it becomes easier and easier. If you can manage to hang in there and negotiate in this new way, however artificial or goofy it seems to you now, after approximately six weeks of doing so, you'll find that what was once new will feel like old hat. So be patient. Put up with the emotional growing pains. You and your relationship will be eternally grateful that you did.

♥ ♥ ♥

AFTERWORD

◇◇◇◇◇◇◇◇◇◇◇◇◇◇◇◇◇◇◇◇◇◇◇◇◇◇◇◇◇◇◇◇◇◇◇◇◇

Declaring a Permanent Truce

This conclusion contains a summary of the main principles outlined in this book. *Warning:* If you're reading this as a shortcut to reading the entire text, this book will self-destruct in three seconds. There are no quick fixes or Band-Aids for curing relationship fighting. You simply need to do the work. You need to learn the skills and techniques I've discussed and practice them until they become part of your bones. I know what I'm suggesting is a pain, but your ongoing efforts will pay off as you soon see your conflicts replaced by connection.

What I want you to retain from Chapter 1, your first Cool-Down step, is that heated exchanges cause ANS arousal and male withdrawal. Male withdrawal results in more heated exchanges, more ANS arousal and withdrawal, and a never-ending downward spiral of fighting. The point to remember is that your interactions must be cooled down before you can hope to achieve a resolution of your conflicts.

The second Cool-Down step, as I explained, is that before you can get control of your fights, you must figure out where you are in the fighting cycle. Stability of Conflict—or the Broken Record phenomenon—is the primary clue that your fighting is out of control.

The third Cool-Down step is to help you identify your Fight Traps and faulty conflict-resolution tactics. You need to remember that these traps and tactics heat the relationship climate, and that no conflict resolution can occur unless they are eliminated.

The fourth Cool-Down step is to resolve chronic sexual fights by teaching your partner to respond to your emotional needs, by understanding the differences between male and female sexuality, and by identifying the nonsexual issues that are being played out in the sexual arena.

Cool-Down step 5 is to recognize that chronic marital fighting is usually caused by unresolved childhood wounds—Old Scars. The form your fights take clues you in to the nature of your Old Scars and the type of healing you need. As you heal your Old Scars within the relationship, you will pave the way for conflict resolution.

Cool-Down step 6 is to train your mind to fight for you, not against you. Your cognitive distortions must be resolved before conflict resolution can occur.

The last Cool-Down step, number 7, is learning and using Relationship Climate Control techniques. The expressive nature of the female gender role ultimately triggers chronic fighting, and the only way to resolve this gender-driven impasse is through the use of these techniques to abort male withdrawal.

At this point, you're ready to begin my conflict-resolution program. You must first acquire good listening skills, avoid the Listening Blunders, and resolve the Listening Blocks that cause them, all discussed in Chapter 8.

The point to retain from Chapter 9 is that before you learn to negotiate, you need to know when *not* to negotiate. Negotiating on inappropriate issues is counterproductive and often the source of greater relationship discord.

And finally, it's time to negotiate a winning contract, but only after you've completed all of the Self-Work tasks I described and know how to introduce your issue for discussion. If a discussion gets off on the wrong foot, it's doomed at the starting gate, and there will be no resolution.

The confronter must also remember to switch to discussion overseer, whose job it is to monitor for signs of ANS arousal and maintain a cool discussion that leads to a mutually satisfactory resolution.

♡

You've finally made it to the finish line! Wipe your sweaty brow. Breathe a sigh of relief and give yourself a pat on the back. You've reached the end . . . and the beginning of a new life and a new relationship. I wish you much happiness and love.

— **Dr. Jamie Turndorf**
(Dr. Love)

♥ ♥ ♥

BIBLIOGRAPHY

◇◇◇

1. Understanding the Chemistry of Fighting

Allen, J. G., and D. M. Haccoun. "Sex Differences in Emotionality: A Multidimensional Approach." *Human Relations* 29 (1976): 711–22.

Averill, J. R. "Studies on Anger and Aggression: Implications for Theories of Emotion." *American Psychologist* 38, no. 11 (1983): 1145–60.

Cannon, W. B. *Bodily Changes in Pain, Hunger, Fear and Rage: An Account of Researches into the Function of Emotional Excitement.* 2nd ed. New York: Appleton-Century-Crofts, 1929.

Gottman, J. M. *Marital Interaction: Experimental Investigations.* New York: Academic Press, 1979.

Gottman, J. M., and R. W. Levenson. "The Social Psychophysiology of Marriage." In *Perspectives on Marital Interaction,* edited by P. Noller and M. A. Fitzpatrick, 182–202. Clevedon, Avon, England: Multilingual Matters, 1988.

Levenson, R. W., and J. M. Gottman. "Marital Interaction: Physiological Linkage and Affective Exchange." *Journal of Personality and Social Psychology* 45 (1983): 587–97.

Liberson, C. W., and W. T. Liberson. "Sex Differences in Autonomic Responses to Electric Shock." *Psychophysiology* 12 (1975): 182–86.

Mornell, P. *Passive Men, Wild Women.* New York: Ballantine Books, 1979.

Napier, A. Y. "The Rejection-Intrusion Pattern: A Central Family Dynamic." *Journal of Marital and Family Therapy* 4 (1978): 5–12.

Notarius, C. I., and J. S. Johnson. "Emotional Expression in Husbands and Wives." *Journal of Marriage and Family* 44 (1982): 483–89.

Notarius, C. I., and R. W. Levenson. "Expressive Tendencies and Physiological Responses to Stress." *Journal of Personality and Social Psychology* 37 (1979): 1204–10.

Roberts, L. J., and L. J. Krokoff. "A Time-Series Analysis of Withdrawal, Hostility, and Displeasure in Satisfied and Dissatisfied Marriages." *Journal of Marriage and Family* 52 (1990): 95–105.

Turndorf, J. "Negative Affect Communication Deficits and the Demand/ Withdraw Negative Escalation Cycle: A Psycho-Physiological Causal Pathway Model." Ph.D. in Psychology diss., California Coast University, 1994.

Van Doornen, L. J. P. "Sex Differences in Physiological Reactions to Real-Life Stress and Their Relationship to Psychological Variables." Paper presented at the 25th annual meeting of the Society for Psychophysiological Research, Houston, Texas, October 1985.

Zillmann, D. *Hostility and Aggression.* Hillsdale, N.J.: Lawrence Erlbaum, 1979.

2. The Relationship Battleground

Ammons, P., and N. Stinnett. "The Vital Marriage: A Closer Look." *Family Relations* 29 (1980): 37–42.

Argyle, M., and A. Furnham. "Sources of Satisfaction and Conflict in Long-Term Relationships." *Journal of Marriage and Family* 45 (1983): 481–93.

Baucom, D. H., and A. N. Adams. "Assessing Communication in Marital Interaction." In *Assessment of Marital Discord,* edited by K. D. O'Leary. Hillsdale, N.J.: Lawrence Erlbaum, 1987.

Billings, A. "Conflict Resolution in Distressed and Nondistressed Married Couples." *Journal of Consulting and Clinical Psychology* 47, no. 2 (1979): 368–76.

Boyd, L. "Interpersonal Communication Skills Differentiating More Satis-fying from Less Satisfying Marital Relationships." Ph.D. diss., Texas A & M University, 1976.

Duck, S. *Relating to Others.* Chicago: Dorsey, 1988.

Feldman, P. "Antagonistic Marriages." *Medical Aspects of Human Sexuality* 19, no. 11 (1985): 149–63.

Gottman, J. M., and N. Silver. *Why Marriages Succeed or Fail . . . And How You Can Make Yours Last.* New York: Simon & Schuster, 1995.

Locke, H. J. *Predicting Adjustment in Marriage: A Comparison of a Divorced and a Happily Married Group.* New York: Henry Holt & Co., 1951.

3. The No-Fly (Off the Handle) Zone

Appel, M. S.; K. A. Holroyd; and L. Gorkin. "Anger and the Etiology and Progression of Physical Illness." In *Emotions in Health and Illness: Theoreti-cal and Research Foundations,* edited by L. Temoshok, C. VanDyke, and L. S. Zegans. New York: Grune and Stratton, 1983.

Berger, C. R. "Social Power and Interpersonal Communication." In *Hand-book of Interpersonal Communication,* edited by M. L. Knapp and G. R. Miller, 439–99. Beverly Hills, CA: Sage, 1985.

Buunk, B., and C. Schaap. "Conflict Resolution Styles Attributed to Self and Partner in Premarital Relationships." *Journal of Social Psychology* 130, no. 6 (1990): 821–23.

Carter, B., and J. K. Peters. *Love, Honor and Negotiate: Making Your Mar-riage Work.* New York: Simon & Schuster, 1996.

Christensen, A. "Detection of Conflict Patterns in Couples." In *Under-standing Major Mental Disorder: The Contribution of Family Interaction Research,* edited by K. Hahlweg and M. J. Goldstein, 250–65. New York: Family Process Press, 1987.

Fitzpatrick, M. A. "A Typological Approach to Marital Interaction." In *Perspectives on Marital Interaction,* 98–120. Clevedon, Avon, England: Multilingual Matters, 1988.

Goldberg, M. "Patterns of Disagreement in Marriage." *Medical Aspects of Human Sexuality* 21, no. 3 (1987): 42–52.

Sullaway, M., and A. Christensen. "Assessment of Dysfunctional Inter-action Patterns in Couples." *Journal of Marriage and Family* 45 (1983): 653–660.

4. Battle of the Bulge

Balswick, J., and C. Peek. "The Inexpressive Male: A Tragedy of American Society." *The Family Coordinator* 20 (1971): 363–68.

Coleman, M., and L. H. Ganong. "Love and Sex Role Stereotypes: Do Macho Men and Feminine Women Make Better Lovers?" *Journal of Personality and Social Psychology* 49 (1985): 170–76.

Jourard, S. M., and P. Lasakow. "Some Factors in Self-Disclosure." *Journal of Abnormal and Social Psychology* 56 (1958): 91–98.

Rubin, L. B. *Intimate Strangers: Men and Women Together.* New York: Harper & Row, 1983.

5. Battle Scars

Bell, E. C., and R. N. Blakeney. "Personality Correlates of Conflict Resolution Modes." *Human Relations* 30 (1977): 849–57.

Bradshaw, J. *Homecoming: Reclaiming and Championing Your Inner Child.* New York: Bantam Books, 1990.

6. How Your Head Can Be Your Own Worst Enemy

Baucom, D. H. "Attributions in Distressed Relations: How Can We Explain Them?" In *Intimate Relationships: Development, Dynamics and Deterioration,* edited by D. Perlman and S. Duck. Beverly Hills, CA: Sage, 1987.

Beck, A. T. *Cognitive Therapy and the Emotional Disorders.* New York: International Universities Press, 1976.

Borysenko, J. *Guilt Is the Teacher, Love Is the Lesson.* New York: Warner Books, 1990.

Burns, D. D. *The Feeling Good Handbook: Using the New Mood Therapy in Everyday Life.* New York: William Morrow, 1989.

7. The Battle-Ax

Gottman, J. M., and L. J. Krokoff. "Marital Interaction and Satisfaction: A Longitudinal View." *Journal of Consulting and Clinical Psychology* 57 (1989): 47–52.

Gottman, J. M., and N. Silver. *Why Marriages Succeed or Fail . . . And How You Can Make Yours Last.* New York: Simon & Schuster, 1995.

Hendrix, H. *Getting the Love You Want.* New York: Henry Holt, 1988.

8. Listening to the Battle Cry

Buck, R. *The Communication of Emotion.* New York: Guilford, 1984.

Buck, R. "Nonverbal Behavior and the Theory of Emotion: The Facial Feedback Hypothesis." *Journal of Personality and Social Psychology* 30 (1980): 811–24.

Jourard, S. M., and P. Lasakow. "Some Factors in Self-Disclosure." *Journal of Abnormal and Social Psychology* 56 (1958): 91–8.

Noller, P. *Nonverbal Communication and Marital Interaction.* New York: Pergamon, 1984.

Pin, E. J., and J. Turndorf. *The Pleasure of Your Company: A Socio-Psychological Analysis of Modern Sociability.* New York: Praeger, 1985.

Schaap, C. *Communication and Adjustment in Marriage.* Lisse, Netherlands: Swets & Zeitlinger, 1982.

Weitz, S. "Sex Differences in Nonverbal Behavior." *Sex Roles* 2, no. 2 (1976): 175–84.

9. On Furlough

Buck, R. *The Communication of Emotion.* New York: Guilford, 1984.

10. The Peace Treaty

Alexander, J. F. "Defensive and Supportive Communications in Family Systems." *Journal of Marriage and Family* 35 (1973): 613–17.

Billings, A. "Conflict Resolution in Distressed and Nondistressed Married Couples." *Journal of Consulting and Clinical Psychology* 47, no. 2 (1979): 368–76.

Folger, J. P., and M. S. Poole. *Working Through Conflict.* Glenview, Ill.: Scott Foresman, 1984.

Gottman, J. M. "Emotional Responsiveness in Marital Conversations." *Journal of Communication* 16 (1982): 108–20.

Hallock, S. "An Understanding of Negotiation Styles Contributes to Effective Reality Therapy for Conflict Resolution with Couples." *Journal of Reality Therapy* 8, no. 1 (1988): 7–12.

Rusbalt, C. E.; D. J. Johnson; and G. D. Morrow. "Impact of Couple Patterns of Problem Solving on Distress and Nondistress in Dating Relationships." *Journal of Personality and Social Psychology* 50 (1986): 744–53.

♥ ♥ ♥

ACKNOWLEDGMENTS

Many thanks to Kathleen Velletri, who scanned the original version of this book for typos (when my eyes could no longer spot them!), and the entire staff of Millbrook Library, who cheerfully assisted in obtaining reference materials.

Above all, I thank all of the patients who have entrusted me with the most intimate aspects of their hearts and lives. I never could have created my conflict-resolution program without you. It is your success stories that I now gratefully share so that millions more may follow in your happy footsteps.

♥ ♥ ♥

ABOUT THE AUTHOR

Known to millions as 'Dr Love' through her website, AskDrLove. com – the Internet's first relationship advice site, launched in 1996 – **Jamie Turndorf PhD** has been delighting readers and audiences for three decades with her engaging blend of professional expertise and humour, and her ability to turn clinical psychobabble into easy-to-understand concepts that transform lives and heal relationships. Her methods have been featured on all major television networks in the United States, including CNN, NBC, CBS, VH1 and FOX, and on WebMD and iVillage. She has also appeared in many top magazines, including *Cosmopolitan, Men's Health* and *Glamour.* In addition, she writes a column called "We Can Work It Out" for *Psychology Today* online. Her *Ask Dr Love* radio show can be heard in Seattle on KKNW and on TalkZone, which broadcasts in 80 countries worldwide.

www.askdrlove.com

HAY HOUSE TITLES OF RELATED INTEREST

YOU CAN HEAL YOUR LIFE, the movie,
starring Louise L. Hay & Friends
(available as a 1-DVD programme and an expanded 2-DVD set)
Watch the trailer at: www.LouiseHayMovie.com

THE SHIFT, the movie,
starring Dr Wayne W. Dyer
(available as a 1-DVD programme and an expanded 2-DVD set)
Watch the trailer at: www.DyerMovie.com

♡

*THE HONEYMOON EFFECT: The Science of Creating
Heaven on Earth,* by Bruce H. Lipton, PhD

*LOVE YOUR ENEMIES: How to Break the Anger Habit and Be a
Whole Lot Happier,* by Sharon Salzberg and Robert Thurman

LOVEABILITY: Knowing How to Love and Be Loved,
by Robert Holden, PhD

*REWIRE YOUR BRAIN FOR LOVE: Creating Vibrant Relationships
Using the Science of Mindfulness,* by Marsha Lucas, PhD

*SECRETS OF ATTRACTION: The Universal Laws of Love,
Sex and Romance,* by Sandra Anne Taylor

*SPIRIT-CENTERED RELATIONSHIPS: Experiencing Greater Love
and Harmony Through the Power of Presencing,*
by Gay Hendricks, PhD, and Kathlyn Hendricks, PhD

All of the above are available at your local bookstore,
or may be ordered by contacting Hay House (see next page).

We hope you enjoyed this Hay House book. If you'd like to
receive our online catalogue featuring additional information on
Hay House books and products, or if you'd like to find out
more about the Hay Foundation, please contact:

Hay House UK, Ltd., Astley House,
33 Notting Hill Gate, London W11 3JQ
Phone: 0-20-3675-2450 • *Fax:* 0-20-3675-2451
www.hayhouse.co.uk • www.hayfoundation.org

Published and distributed in the United States by: Hay House, Inc., P.O.
Box 5100, Carlsbad, CA 92018-5100
Phone: (760) 431-7695 or (800) 654-5126
Fax: (760) 431-6948 or (800) 650-5115
www.hayhouse.com®

Published and distributed in Australia by: Hay House Australia Pty. Ltd.,
18/36 Ralph St., Alexandria NSW 2015 • *Phone:* 612-9669-4299
Fax: 612-9669-4144 • www.hayhouse.com.au

Published and distributed in the Republic of South Africa by:
Hay House SA (Pty), Ltd., P.O. Box 990, Witkoppen 2068
Phone/Fax: 27-11-467-8904 • www.hayhouse.co.za

Published in India by: Hay House Publishers India, Muskaan
Complex, Plot No. 3, B-2, Vasant Kunj, New Delhi 110 070
Phone: 91-11-4176-1620 • *Fax:* 91-11-4176-1630 • www.hayhouse.co.in

Distributed in Canada by: Raincoast Books, 2440 Viking Way,
Richmond, B.C. V6V 1N2 • *Phone:* 1-800-663-5714
Fax: 1-800-565-3770 • www.raincoast.com

Take Your Soul on a Vacation

Visit www.HealYourLife.com® to regroup, recharge,
and reconnect with your own magnificence.
Featuring blogs, mind-body-spirit news, and
life-changing wisdom from Louise Hay and friends.